FOR YOUR
CONSIDERATION

Dwayne
"The Rock"
Johnson

This one is for Kerin. Thanks for letting me be your Swayze. It's also for Mom and Dad because legally if your parents help you with student loans you have to dedicate your first book to them.

Library of Congress Cataloging in Publication Number: 2019936800
ISBN: 978-1-68369-149-5

Printed in the United States of America

Typeset in Century, Adobe Caslon Pro, and Avenir

Text by Tres Dean
Cover and interior designed by Aurora Parlegreco
Cover illustration by Mercedes deBellard
Interior illustrations by Ben Mounsey-Wood
Production management by John J. McGurk

Quirk Books
215 Church Street
Philadelphia, PA 19106
quirkbooks.com

10 9 8 7 6 5 4 3 2 1

FOR YOUR CONSIDERATION

Dwayne "The Rock" Johnson

Tres Dean

QUIRK BOOKS
PHILADELPHIA

Table of Contents

Introduction

I love The Rock.

Hardly a hot take, right? Everybody loves The Rock. I don't think my mom has ever seen one of his movies but my mom loves The Rock—which, to be fair, might be because he's objectively a hunk for the ages. There are plenty of reasons to love him. He's a compelling movie star, a once-in-a-lifetime fitness icon, and an endlessly likable guy offscreen.

The Rock's career in Hollywood spans two decades, and he enjoyed a monumentally important stint as a pro wrestler that included reigns as the WWF/WWE, Intercontinental, and Tag Team Champion as well as multiple WrestleMania main events. He helped reinvigorate the fading *Fast & Furious* movie franchise, cofounded the juggernaut film studio Seven Bucks Productions, and took over the world of television with his smash HBO show *Ballers*. Alongside his wrestling archrival Stone Cold Steve Austin, he defined one of the most beloved eras of the sport's history. The Rock has been a rare cultural constant for the past several years. We don't have many real movie stars anymore, performers whose presence can guarantee a film's success even if a franchise isn't attached. And many film icons of the past have gone on to disappoint us either professionally (Ben Affleck) or in their personal lives (also Ben Affleck). Where others have faltered or stumbled, The Rock has always managed to succeed. His personal life is free of controversy and his filmography, though not free of bombs, has managed to thrive.

Between the extent of his fame and the length of his career, there's a whole lot of ground to cover in this book. Ultimately, I want to answer a simple question: Why do we love Dwayne "The Rock" Johnson so much?

Because it matters, doesn't it? Not everybody has what it takes to become a cultural icon, and when someone does, it says just as much about the fans as it does about the individual. The Rock's life story is fascinating and he's fun to watch in movies, but you could say the same of a litany of other actors. A great smile and easygoing charm aren't enough to guarantee success. We, the fans, the general public, are the ones who elevate our icons. They cannot be bought or built. They have to prove themselves worthy of our adoration. Our motivations for giving our support to public figures and the reasons we feel compelled to do so are worth scrutinizing. What do these people mean to us? What does the fact that they mean something to us say about us?

Over the course of five essays (and some fun detours exploring some of the goofier corners of The Rock's history, we'll look at how The Rock has come to occupy the space he does in pop culture today. We'll examine the ways he differentiates himself from other movie stars and how those choices influence our perception of him. Not all of it is going to be breezy—we'll also explore inequality, poverty, and the fallacy of the American dream. Not what you expected from a book about a former pro wrestler and current action movie star, huh? That's because The Rock isn't just an ex-wrestler or a cut-and-dried action hero. He embodies the spirit of resilience, of refusing to let failure keep you from achieving your dreams. He's living proof that hard work pays off and that, even if the deck is systemically stacked against you, there's a way to rise above your circumstances.

Don't get me wrong, though. This book is not going to be a Sociology 101 lecture. The Rock is, above all else, a fun performer. Hopefully some of that energy is captured here as we talk about legendary fistfights, his obsession with Elvis Presley, and the time he guest-starred as himself on *Wizards of Waverly Place*.

It's important to understand beforehand that his body of work will be judged on a more complex metric than traditional "good vs. bad." An equally important guiding principle is the Rock Movie Metric, or the difference between a Rock movie and a movie that The Rock is in.

Is *Moana* a better movie than, say, *Skyscraper*? Of course. *Moana* is a better movie in almost every conceivable way than the entirety of The Rock's filmography. It's beautifully animated, it's got that signature Disney heart, and Dwayne "The Rock" Johnson sings a song written by Lin-Manuel Miranda. *Moana* is perfect.

But *Moana* is not a Dwayne "The Rock" Johnson movie. It's not just because The Rock isn't the star or because it's an animated film. No, *Moana* lacks the signature elements of a classic Rock movie.

This nebulous concept is difficult to define and we can't pretend there aren't exceptions. That said, a proper Rock movie must contain some, if not all, of the following elements:

- One (1) fistfight
- One (1) explosion
- Three (3) gratuitous shots of The Rock's absolutely jacked-as-hell upper body
- One (1) scene in which The Rock fights something that until that moment we have never seen him fight (i.e., earthquake, giant wolf, Vin Diesel)
- One (1) feat of strength (i.e., leaping from a construction rig onto a skyscraper, flexing so hard the cast on his arm shatters)
- One (1) smolder

By this metric, *Moana* is not a Rock movie but *Rampage* is. *Pain & Gain*? Oddly enough, not a Rock movie. *The Scorpion King*? The original Rock movie. The Rock Movie Metric is less an indicator of quality and more an indicator of content and tone. This book will largely discuss and judge Rock movies, though movies that The Rock is in will not be ignored. Rest assured that yes, *Moana* is great, and no, its greatness is not being overlooked as we move toward our grand unified theory of Dwayne "The Rock" Johnson.

A word on spoilers: there will be some. If you're particularly precious about not finding out who has a surprise cameo at the end of *Central Intelligence* or how the fight between Dom and Hobbs in *Fast Five* ends, proceed with caution.

PART I

The Rock and the Evolution of the American Action Star

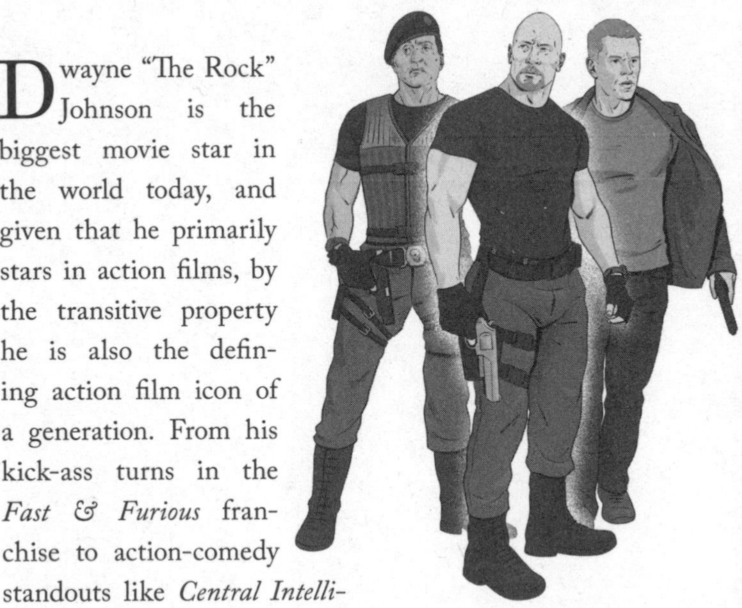

Dwayne "The Rock" Johnson is the biggest movie star in the world today, and given that he primarily stars in action films, by the transitive property he is also the defining action film icon of a generation. From his kick-ass turns in the *Fast & Furious* franchise to action-comedy standouts like *Central Intelligence* and *Jumanji: Welcome to the Jungle*, he's the apex of what the genre has to offer in this day and age. If an action star's merit is judged by the number of things they have punched, literally and metaphorically, The Rock is the first to have punched the holy trinity of Vin Diesel, a giant monster, and an earthquake. Top that, Wahlberg.

Still, The Rock's rise to the top of the genre is no happy

accident. Certainly he has worked tremendously hard both on-screen and off, but it's also worth noting that The Rock is the perfect action star for this generation, for this moment in time. No amount of hard work can propel someone to the top if the top isn't a place they're meant to occupy. Need proof? When was the last time you rushed to the theater to see a Sam Worthington movie?

Dwayne "The Rock" Johnson is the biggest action star of a generation because he's everything this generation wants—nay, needs—in an action star. More than just a celebrity, he is a man who epitomizes generational values. The state of the American action star has steadily evolved over decades, and what that role is today is one The Rock is uniquely suited to fill. To understand this, you have to go back to the beginning—or at least to the '80s.

If you want to understand a moment of history, to see in the most potent form possible what a collective consciousness was feeling at a specific point in time, look to the fiction that culture produced in that moment. Fiction can articulate a mass sentiment, a movement, or a cultural shift in ways nothing else can. Journalism and documentary may speak to fact better than fiction, but fiction can convey a feeling like no other medium. This fact isn't limited to highbrow art. Horror is often lauded as the cornerstone of genre storytelling that best articulates generational anxieties, for instance. The slasher film boom started by *Psycho* in 1960 and continued in the '70s by *The Texas Chainsaw Massacre*, *Halloween*, and their contemporaries taps into not a mass lust for violence but rather fears stemming from the Vietnam War. An entire generation of American men flew halfway around the world to witness a senseless mass of carnage and violence at the behest of powerful men whose interests were hardly aligned with those of the soldiers on the ground. These men came home irreparably changed. The slasher years articulated the generational fear of suddenly living in the midst of traumatized men who knew how to kill with intense brutality.

Science fiction's ability to speak to the cultural moment is also widely accepted as fact. From *Planet of the Apes*'s bold warning that to tease nuclear war was to tempt the wrath of whatever gods there might be, to the way Alex Garland's 2018 masterpiece *Annihilation* beautifully articulates the fear that trauma changes humans in primal, genetic ways, it's been quite some time since the genre was derided as mindless pulp.

Action, though? To most viewers, it's still pure escapism. Movies about men and women shooting guns, driving fast cars, and busting skulls tend to be chalked up to, at best, just a good time. To be fair, few action films aspire to more than that. Still, art reflects culture, whether it means to or not. Just because action movies tend to prioritize explosion innovation over thematic subtext doesn't mean they don't contain, well, thematic subtext.

At the forefront of this genre is the action star. It's a storied position, one that lacks an equivalent in horror and sci fi (horror has scream queens but they're often created through repetition rather than audience demand). An action star is an actor, almost always a man, whose name sells an action movie. He is the draw, not the plot or director. Look at any list of great action stars and you'll find some of the most famous, highest-grossing celebrities of all time. Jason Statham. Bruce Willis. Jackie Chan. All legends. All icons whose work regularly defines and redefines the action film genre. Crucially, all actors who define the public conception of what a man is.

That's the cultural zeitgeist action movies speak to: masculinity. To track the evolution of action stars is to track over generations the shifting idealization of masculinity, which is perennially embodied by the action star of the moment. This tradition began with genre forebearers like John Wayne and Steve McQueen, but the modern action star was born in the 1980s, thanks to two individuals: Sylvester Stallone and Arnold Schwarzenegger.

The latter is perhaps as clear-cut an action star as there's ever been, a former bodybuilder resembling mythical Übermensch more than mere mortal. Sporting biceps bigger than John Wayne's head, Schwarzenegger won seven Mr. Olympia titles and three pro Mr. Universes. His debut as an action icon came in 1982, in the film *Conan the Barbarian*. A cinematic adaptation of Robert E. Howard's legendary pulp character, Conan is a rugged icon of raw masculinity. He's a sword-swinging, ripped-as-hell barbarian king, made just as famous by the paintings of fantasy icon Frank Frazetta, which adorned Howard's novels, as by the stories they told.

Few human men have resembled the ultra-idealized portrait of unbridled masculinity depicted by Frazetta. Arnold is one such man.

Although he portrayed the legendary Cimmerian only once more, in 1984's *Conan the Destroyer*, most every project in which Schwarzenegger starred in the years that followed channeled the same machismo. From *Commando*'s John Matrix to *Predator*'s Dutch, Schwarzenegger's forte was ridiculously idealized macho men with ridiculous names to match.

Stallone's portrayals of masculinity would prove just as over-the-top, though his journey to those roles was far less direct. Two of Sly's most iconic characters, Rocky Balboa and John Rambo (arguably the most iconic action role of all time), are rooted in what someone who doesn't fully respect the craft of action movies might call artistry. Rocky and Rambo may be regarded today as avatars of cinematic masculinity, but they didn't start out that way. *Rocky* and *First Blood* paint, respectively, a portrait of realistic and warm masculinity (as opposed to the heightened, often toxic forms it takes in other '80s classics) and a deconstruction of the havoc that war and violence can wreak on the soul.

Only through countless sequels, which often led to diminishing returns in quality, do the characters become clichés. Rambo becomes the very action hero the character originally deconstructed; Rocky singlehandedly wins the Cold War via a boxing match with a Russian super-robot. (Dolph Lundgren's character, Ivan Drago, is not a literal robot, but Rocky has a literal robot sidekick in that movie, and if that's not an action trope, nothing is.) Soon Sly was every bit the stereotype Arnold was. Characters like Cobra from the movie *Cobra* (you've gotta wonder if the title came before the character with this one) and Ray Tango of *Tango and Cash* are the shredded one-liner-dropping clichés you'd expect from an action movie made before 1990.

Plenty of peers and imitators soon arose. The aforementioned Lundgren has had a healthy career and falls in the same "unspeakably large muscle boy" category as Sly and Arnold. Though not of the same physical stature, Jean-Claude Van Damme and Chuck Norris blended the grace of Eastern martial arts with the grit of American action movies, becoming icons in the same ballpark but playing different positions from the (literal) big guys.

That these movies and characters fit a certain mold isn't to say they are inherently bad, mind you. Anyone who besmirches the good name of *Predator* doesn't love action movies, and even some of the more tired portrayals are iconic in their own right. Stallone's "This is where the law stops and I start" line in *Cobra* is about as perfect as action movies get. The point is that action heroes of the '70s and '80s were embodied in a specific way—one that, for better or for worse, epitomized what the culture at the time valued in masculinity. Physicality was paramount; if you didn't *look* like the toughest man on the planet, you'd better be able to make a strong case for the title by possessing insane martial arts abilities. Internally, many of these characters are as cartoonish as their physiques.

Intense heteronormativity is another facet of these characters. They always have a love interest who often is a thinly written woman in need of saving by the time the film's third act rolls around, never so much a character as a plot device and a massive billboard reminding you that this action hero *has sex—with WOMEN.*

Why did audiences of this era value self-serious bodybuilder tough guys so deeply? The 1980s saw the Cold War wither and die, but even in that conflict's final years American exceptionalism was at an all-time high. Action stars mimicked reality—they had to represent the ideal American male specimen. These characters couldn't be scrappy underdogs or everymen who relied on wits over brute strength. No, you had to know immediately upon seeing them that they could break every damn Commie out there in half with their bare hands.

Eventually the Cold War came to a close and geopolitical tensions lessened for the first time in decades. The times, they were a-changin', and the American action star followed suit.

Die Hard's hero John McClane, played by Bruce Willis, debuted in 1988 and is another contender for most iconic action character of all time. While he has the cool-guy grit and machismo of the Lundgrens and Stallones before him, he has the body of a guy who looks like he covers your kid's carpool on Tuesdays and Fridays. Willis presented moviegoers with the first action icon in ages who looked like them. McClane isn't a lethal military commando or a martial arts savant. He's a cop who's in the wrong place at the wrong time and survives the movie through resourcefulness and dumb luck over brute strength and seemingly bulletproof skin.

A year prior, *Lethal Weapon* introduced audiences to Martin Riggs and Roger Murtaugh, an odd-couple cop duo featuring Danny Glover as Murtaugh, the now-archetypal, by-the-books straight man, and Mel Gibson as Riggs, a suicidal loose cannon who, as they say, doesn't play by the rules. Riggs and Murtaugh are, like John McClane, salt-of-the-earth dudes with families and everyday responsibilities who end up in over their heads on what at first appears to be a routine homicide investigation. They're scrappy and stubborn more than superhuman.

Riggs, Murtaugh, and McClane introduced audiences to action heroes that possessed all the bombast of Sly and Arnold but also a degree of realism. The time for idealized physiques and tough-guy shenanigans was ending. The next generation of action stars was far more self-deprecating, funnier, and more authentic, but, more important, they seemed more familiar—even if, like Gibson's Riggs, they had better hair than you.

These characters paved the way for the action star of the nineties, starring in a bevy of wildly successful sequels. Unlike the eighties, which were dominated by Stallone and Schwarzenegger, the nineties had no single definitive action star. Instead, a number of actors rose to the top, each bringing something unique to the table.

One standout of this decade was Will Smith. After getting his start on the hit television comedy *The Fresh Prince of Bel-Air* he strung together a series of hit films, including *Bad Boys*, *Independence Day*, and *Men in Black*, that cemented him not only as a once-in-a-generation action icon but also as one of the biggest stars in the world (honestly, of all time).

Like Willis before him, Smith was far from a physical specimen. He was in shape, sure, but the guy wasn't going to take home a Mr. Olympia trophy. Rather, Smith presented a sort of everyman cranked up a few notches. He was tall but on the skinny side, and even when he was particularly fit, his physique seemed attainable to string-bean kids in the audience. No secret Charles Atlas serum ordered from the back of an old comic book would be required to look like him.

Still, unlike Sly and Arnold, Smith's physique and good looks weren't his primary draw. Smith was a charmer. He could act. He could play the straight man in *Bad Boys* just as deftly as the goofball in *Men in Black*. He had chemistry with everyone and, despite his unmistakable star quality, still gave off the vibe that you could grab a beer with him.

Other actors embodied the elevated everyman that populated action cinema in the nineties. Stars like Keanu Reeves and, yes, Bruce Willis kept the fire burning in films like *Point Break*, *The Matrix*, *Armageddon*, and the *Die Hard* sequels. Characters like Neo, Johnny Utah, and Harry Stamper thrived in this peaceful era, when America was hardly immune to foreign conflict but was not embroiled in some generation-defining great war. In the nineties, the action star became a reflection more than an aspiration. These characters weren't elite special forces agents or trained mercenaries. They were cops, farmers, blue-collar guys in whom men could see themselves, only a little bit funnier and minus fifteen pounds or so.

This trend changed rather abruptly in 2001. The events of September 11 and the subsequent war in the Middle East burned America's self-perception to the ground. No longer was there room for joy in action cinema, only reflection on what remained in the wake of this monumental shift. This was not an era in which cooler heads prevailed. This was an era of revenge, petty and violent and ugly. Only an era like this could birth Jack Bauer and Jason Bourne.

Although *24*'s Jack Bauer is a television character, he deserves mention in this discussion because he was an action star for America's age of fear. (The elevation of television in the late nineties and early aughts, and where the action star stands in that evolution, is a whole 'nother essay.) Portrayed by Kiefer Sutherland, Bauer is technically ahead of his time. The series, which had been filmed before September 11, premiered just a few short weeks later, on November 6. It proved a smash hit after its first season, which, upon rewatch, doesn't read nearly as jingoistic as those that followed.

The show follows Bauer, the foremost field agent of the fictional Counter Terrorism Unit (CTU), an organization that targeted solely the hyperspecific (yet technically vague) concept of terrorism. He serves as America's proverbial right hand, exacting brutal justice on countless nameless extremists serving a litany of causes. They are almost always of the Middle Eastern origins, though the Russians are in the mix at various points as well. (Can't have a hypervigilant American action hero who doesn't take down some commies.)

Bauer is both human weapon and family man, a wholly unrealistic cocktail. He's the Punisher without the dead family (in season one, at least). In an era in which America feared nothing but the brutal faceless specter of terrorism, Bauer served as an analogue through which viewers could vicariously appreciate the efficient, visceral slaughter of men who represented real-life villains.

The rise of Matt Damon's Jason Bourne began one year after Bauer's debut. Bourne was a slightly more complex character. A former government agent, he struggles with amnesia and a whole lot of faceless, nameless government agents chasing after him. Over the course of three movies he rediscovers and grapples with his complicated past and, eventually, exacts vengeance on the people who made him a human weapon.

Unlike Bauer, not all the villains Bourne fights are terrorists; many are sinister black-ops agents of the U.S. government. As the early aughts passed, Americans lost faith in the institutions that held up their nation. As revelations of torture, war crimes, and government corruption emerged, the only thing Americans grew to fear almost as much as terrorism was their own government. Bauer and Bourne provided the country with two icons through which they could confront their fear of the enemy overseas and the enemy at home.

The ethic of these characters seeped into all facets of action cinema, leading to a slew of knockoffs that today read more like state-sponsored propaganda than action movies. It even found its way into superhero movies, such as the acclaimed 2008 film *The Dark Knight*. The story pits Christian Bale's Batman against Heath Ledger's Joker, who shares far more with real-life terrorists than Jack Nicholson's and Cesar Romero's campy comic-book takes on the character. There's also a blatant Patriot Act analogue utilized by Batman in the film's third act. The depiction of a superhero grappling with ethical quandaries regarding surveillance, terrorism, and morality was a rare capture of lightning in a bottle that Warner Bros. and DC Comics spent years afterward trying to re-create, only to fail time and time again.

The following summer director Kathryn Bigelow's *The Hurt Locker* hit theaters. Although far from the first movie to take a hard, critical look at what America's War on Terror was doing to the people fighting it, it was by far the most acclaimed and most effective. The glimpse into the brutal life of a bomb squad deployed to the Middle East spoke to the exhaustion of the moment and made Bigelow the first woman to take home a Best Director win at the Academy Awards. (The film also won for Best Picture.)

The Hurt Locker may not be a cut-and-dried action movie but it spoke to the current state of the genre, whether it meant to or not. The time for childishly serious things had passed.

It's here that our hero joins the story. As years passed, *24* faded from the public consciousness and Matt Damon stepped away from the Bourne franchise. The winds of change were blowing. American film audiences no longer wanted grim reminders of the evil outside their doors. They wanted—nay, needed—to escape. They needed bombast. They needed a hero.

They needed Dwayne "The Rock" Johnson.

By 2011 America was ten years removed from the genesis of the War on Terror. Social media had revolutionized communication and allowed perceptions of gender, race, and masculinity to evolve faster than ever before. No longer was the apex of masculinity a ripped white dude who beat up nonwhite people (often coded simply as "terrorists"). No longer were action movies expected to address America's decade-long struggles overseas or serve as a coping mechanism for those conflicts.

Escapism was very much back in. The Marvel Cinematic Universe was under way and thriving, Kesha and Lady Gaga had made it totally cool to unironically love pop music, and (for better or worse) the *Twilight* movies were a worldwide phenomenon. A trip to the movie theater no longer required American audiences to meditate on their nation's sins. It instead offered stakes-free explosions, melodramatic romance, and maybe a dirty joke or two. Ultimately, it meant the best of both worlds—action stars with the bombast of the eighties and the lighthearted self-awareness of the nineties. The Rock's time had come.

His revelatory appearance in 2011's *Fast Five* proved a lightning-rod moment for his career, showing audiences what he was capable of with a good script and a talented director to guide him. The American moviegoing public was finally ready to receive what The Rock had to offer. Through his appearances in the Fast & Furious franchise and a bevy of other massive blockbusters like *San Andreas*, *Skyscraper*, and *Jumanji: Welcome to the Jungle* he has been the single most crucial figure when it comes to defining what an action star is—and means—in the twenty-first century.

It is imperative to mention that The Rock is biracial and multiethnic; his Samoan mother grew up in Hawaii and his black father was raised in Nova Scotia. Undeniably, in the past several decades a performer's race has been fundamental to the opportunities they've been offered, both inside and outside the action genre. The Stallones, Schwarzeneggers, Bauers, and Bournes who came before him? They're all white. The unfortunate reality is that because these characters were the proverbial strong arms of America in their time, their whiteness was an asset. In the eyes of many white American viewers, the nation's greatest weapon against fictional terrorism couldn't have been anything other than Caucasian.

Thankfully, times have changed. Modern audiences are demanding that heroes represent them accurately, which in this case means not being exclusively white. That The Rock, a man of multiples races and ethnicities, occupies the action hero space is groundbreaking. His film career both speaks to and is a result of how far representation in media has come. And though there's still much progress to be made, it's hard not to enjoy the moment.

The Rock's action characters are almost always family men. Their efforts to save the world aren't rooted in duty to country or desire for revenge so much as they are born out of the desire to protect loved ones. No matter the size of the threat, family comes first. Even Hobbs from *Fast & Furious* and Roadblock from *G. I. Joe: Retaliation* (military men driven by duty) are fathers who have warm, loving relationships with their wives and children. Their families are more than just bodies to be kidnapped by the bad guys, more than hollow motivation for the star to punch things and shoot guns. Rather, family relationships lend warmth and depth to The Rock's characters, grounding them in a relatable human experience even if the man himself is the polar opposite of an everyman.

The action in these movies is huge, cartoonish even. You won't find a third-rate Jason Bourne shaky-cam rig in a Rock movie. No, you'll find the star throwing nuclear torpedoes with his bare hands, fighting submarines and giant monsters, and leaping from a massive construction rig into a single open window in a building thousands of feet from the ground. Action in The Rock's movies is *fun*. It's not grossly violent or true to life. It's overtly playful and prioritizes entertainment and thrill. After all, you know The Rock is going to win.

In fact, the star said in a 2018 *Rolling Stone* interview that the film gigs he takes must satisfy a rule: always send the audience home happy. The Rock doesn't do films with sad endings. You can trust that no matter how many punches he takes, no matter how many gunfights he's caught in, he's going to come out fine. Rock movies always have a happy ending.

You'd think that this knowledge would defuse tension in his films, but you'd be wrong. Rather, it provides the audience a sort of assurance. "Come on this journey with me," he says, "and no matter how bad things get, I promise you'll leave in a good mood." These days, that kind of guarantee is rare. With Rock movies, you know what you're getting—but in the best way.

Action cinema has shifted both in and out of sync with the rise of The Rock. All the stars of box-office hits these days are formidable forces who have contributed to a shift in the genre and catered to the changing demands of audiences.

You can't talk about modern action stars without addressing the Chris in the room—well, the four Chrises. Chrises Evans, Hemsworth, Pratt, and Pine collectively form a formidable force in modern Hollywood. Three have appeared in the multibillion-dollar box-office phenomenon that is the Marvel Cinematic Universe (the exception is Pine, who costarred in DC's *Wonder Woman*), and they have dominated other heavy-hitting franchises including *Jurassic Park, Star Trek,* and *Ghostbusters*. The Chrises are a combined cinematic force to be reckoned with, and, similar to The Rock, they mostly inhabit modern ideals of nontoxic masculinity.

Chris Evans is a real-life superhero, using his platform to champion social justice causes and to do cute stuff like adopt dogs and help Regina King up the stairs after she wins an Oscar. It almost makes you forgive him for being a New England Patriots fan. Hemsworth is entirely content with being a hot Australian dad-bro offscreen. It seems like all the guy does when he's not shooting is surf with his kids and cook with his wife. Pine almost seems to regret his movie-star good looks and leading-man charisma, taking every weird, unsettling, and often hilarious role that studios throw at him between blockbuster hits. (He's quietly the funniest of the four, as evidenced by his appearance in *Wet Hot American Summer: First Day of Camp.*) Pratt leaves a bit to be desired offscreen, but two of his most famous characters, Star-Lord from *Guardians of the Galaxy* and Emmet from *The Lego Movie,* provide interesting critiques of modern action heroes and insight into audiences' perceptions of them.

Still, regardless of box office performance and overall fame, the four Chrises remain ever so slightly in the shadow of The Rock. Which has less to do with talent than with the fact that the foursome's fame is tied to a handful of specific, established characters that they embody. Chris Evans is as talented as Hollywood leading men come, but to most of the moviegoing public he will always be Captain America. Hemsworth has taken a number of fascinating projects outside of action, from *Bad Times at the El Royale* to *The Cabin in the Woods* (he may be the Chris for whom a future Oscar is most likely), but he will always be known best for playing Thor. Pratt and Pine are in similar predicaments, their legacies perpetually tied to an established intellectual property with which they've been associated.

This isn't to say that The Rock hasn't also been tied to some incredibly prominent IP. He's appeared in plenty of video game movies and established franchises. But he has never starred as a character who is already more famous than he is. The Rock makes his characters, not vice versa. He, not Luke Hobbs or Dr. Smolder Bravestone, is the draw. As much as we may love the Chrises, we can't always say the same for them.

If there's a single action performer in Hollywood today who can make the best case for the most iconic, beloved action star over The Rock, it's probably Tom Cruise. Cruise's *Mission: Impossible* franchise is, like *Fast & Furious*, the rare series that gets better with every installment. After 2018's critically acclaimed *Mission: Impossible – Fallout* the franchise's stock has never been higher—nor has Cruise as an action icon. His career spans decades and genres. He's a versatile leading man who's had it all: big-budget action like *Top Gun* and the original *Mission: Impossible* as well as award-winning hits like *Jerry Maguire* and *Born on the Fourth of July*. Since the mid-aughts he has almost entirely stuck to action movies, most of which are good and many of which are great. Even the mediocre ones don't fail at the box office. Over thirty years into his career Cruise is still a movie star with nearly unparalleled box office draw.

Like The Rock, whose reputation suffered in the mid-aughts thanks to a series of lousy roles in lousy movies, Cruise experienced a career dip around the same time. The difference is that Cruise's nadir had less to do with the quality of his films than with his personal life. Between jumping on Oprah's couch and appearing in a promotional video for Scientology in which he comes off as utterly deranged, his personal brand took quite a hit. To this day, more than a decade of good PR and good behavior later, these events are the stuff of pop culture legend, and many people still regard him as that crazy Scientologist. It's hard to fault them for it. The details of Cruise's personal life are a public-relations Pandora's box. Once those demons are out in the open, they're never going to be hidden again. As a result, the public might still love Tom Cruise the actor but they hold little affection for Tom Cruise the person.

The Rock comes out on top. Even after that string of misses in the middle of his career, today he's one of the only action stars in the business who can draw the masses into theaters for a movie not based on a comic book or film franchise. He doesn't come with a closet so full of skeletons that we can see a couple of femurs peeking out from behind the door. He's easy to love both on- and offscreen, and it sure doesn't hurt that he's excellent at pretending to beat up bad dudes while cameras film him.

The identity of the American action star will always be in flux. The man who is a generational icon one day might find himself starring in *Kindergarten Cop* the next. The mark of a truly great action star is one who knows his moment and, when it comes, seizes it. Unfortunately, The Rock won't always be the action star we need. Times change. The needs of audiences will inevitably evolve and indeed are already doing so; it's hard to imagine that the next great American action star will be male, and Charlize Theron's rise through the genre's ranks since *Mad Max: Fury Road* suggests that she is next in line to the throne. But for now we are lucky to have The Rock. He knows what we want—nay, what we need—and he gives it to us. He knows that these days, we just want to escape. He'll always send us home happy.

THE ROCK SAYS:
A Definitive Ranking of The Rock's Catchphrases

The Rock is the greatest talker in the history of pro wrestling. Keep your Stone Cold Steve Austins and your "Rowdy" Roddy Pipers. The Rock could out-talk them all with his jaw wired shut and a bronchial infection on top of that. He understands the psychology of performing pro wrestling better than most, but it's what he says in front of those crowds that has cemented his legend. He creates thunderous poetry, seemingly inventing a new language as he bends and twists the rules of English grammar. Heck, *Webster's* (the best of all the dictionaries!) even added "smackdown" to the dictionary in 2007.

The Rock has a greater repertoire of catchphrases than any other pro wrestler, newscaster, superhero, or fictional character. Not every one is perfect, but even his lesser lines are lesser due more to context than weakness. They function far better in combination, like a veritable verbal *Street Fighter* combo, than on their own. What follows is the definitive list of those slogans, their definitions, and their ranking in the Grand Oeuvre of Rock Catchphrases.

14. "Who in the blue hell are you?"

Not much of a catchphrase, just a valid question to ask given that 90 percent of professional wrestlers are identical buff white dudes with long hair.

13. "The Rock says . . . "

On the one hand, no great Rock monologue is complete without a sentence that starts with "The Rock says . . . " On the other, this phrase is dull on its own. Which is not to say it's a bad catchphrase! It's genuinely iconic, even when included on its own as a soundbite in The Rock's entrance music. But it's a modifier, not a full-fledged catchphrase.

12. "Just bring it."

This is the phrase that has perhaps been most heavily incorporated into The Rock's branding. It's not a particularly unique catchphrase and has more impact in print than it does spoken aloud (and even in print it can come off as a weird hyper-aggressive fitness slogan).

11. The Rock: "The millions."
The audience: "AND MILLIONS!"

This would be a top five catchphrase if it never developed past its initial incarnation. The Rock began using this one when he was at his peak as a wrestling villain and easily the most hated guy on the roster. He'd refer to his "millions AND MILLIONS" of fans to a chorus of heated boos. Genius stuff. As audiences fell more in love with him, it became a call and response, with The Rock starting the phrase and the audience finishing it. It's a cool bit, but it's nowhere near as great as The Rock trolling an arena of thousands ferociously jeering him.

10. "Roody-poo candy-ass"

This is a general insult that The Rock would toss at any given opponent. It's half great: the "roody-poo" feels corny today but The Rock calling someone a "candy-ass" is still solid gold and improves any great Rock quote or monologue.

9. "Take ______. Shine it up real nice. And stick it right up your candy ass!"

Remember how any great Rock quote is instantly improved by the inclusion of the term "candy-ass"? Case in point.

8. "FINALLY, THE ROCK HAS COME BACK TO ______!"

The standard opening to any great Rock appearance, punctuated by the name of the city in which he's performing. Iconic but beholden to formula—it only works in that single context of an introduction. "FINALLY, THE ROCK HAS COME BACK TO ANAHEIM!" sounds great in the moment but it's hardly something you want to yell at your friends on the playground before hitting them with a People's Elbow.

7. "You will go one-on-one with the Great One."

When The Rock dropped this one, he meant business. The time for quips and verbal barbs had passed. The time for violence had arrived. Whoever was on the receiving end of this one, best have made peace with whatever gods they believed in, because you don't go one-on-one with the Great One, the Brahma Bull, the People's Champion, and come out unscathed.

6. "Lay the smackdown!"

In terms of cultural ramifications, this is the big one. The Rock wasn't the first wrestler to use the term *smackdown* but he's certainly the one responsible for popularizing it to the point that not only did World Wrestling Entertainment (WWE) create a show called *SmackDown Live* in 1999 but *Webster's* added it to the dictionary. It's a real word now because of him. You can type it into Microsoft Word and it won't get underlined in red! Thanks, Mr. Rock.

5. "Layeth the smackethdown!"

Same as above but utilized when The Rock was feeling . . . theatrical? Fancy? Honestly, who cares why? It's such a good twist on the line. Pro wrestling felt Shakespearean for a split second when he dropped this one, and the WWE needed a touch of class in the '90s.

4. "IT DOESN'T MATTER _____!"

An interjection lobbed at anyone who dared to cross The Rock. Relentlessly versatile, it includes variations, such as "It doesn't matter what your name is!" and "It doesn't matter what you think!" Perhaps most impressive is how subtly

The Rock could bait this trap, asking a seemingly honest question and cutting off his opponent a couple of words into their answer. This is also the catchphrase that got the most kids in trouble in the '90s. No parent takes well to being told, "IT DOESN'T MATTER WHAT TIME I'M SUPPOSED TO GO TO BED!"

3. "Know your role and shut your mouth!"

The ego on display here is both stunning and beautiful. "Know your role" is such a cold, demeaning thing to say to someone mouthing off to you—a true power move. Arrogance was crucial to The Rock's persona as a pro wrestler and it's never more apparent or present than in this phrase.

2. "Jabroni"

The rare solitary noun in The Rock's catchphrase arsenal. Just an effortlessly effective insult that packs more punch than most wrestlers' entire catchphrase arsenals. The term has roots in wrestling lingo as a name for someone who is scripted to lose regularly, so technically we can't credit The Rock with its creation. However, he's the man who made it iconic. In his hands it's a versatile and transcendent insult with plenty of real-world application. Seriously, call someone a jabroni to their face. They won't say anything. They can't.

1. "IF YA SMELL WHAT THE ROCK IS COOKIN'."

The big one. The undisputed GOAT of The Rock catchphrases and easily the most quotable. Grammatically speaking, it's not so much a legitimate inquiry as it is a statement or rhetorical question, effectively translating to "You know what I mean?" It's the ultimate punctuation to a Rock monologue. The gusto with which he delivers it, the heavily calculated pacing of the line . . . it all makes for a perfect catchphrase, one that never has been and never will be topped in professional wrestling. We smell it, Rocky. We always have.

PART II

Dwayne "The Rock" Johnson and Modern Masculinity

Men with calves the size of California redwoods aren't supposed to talk about their feelings. Not to discredit the unbelievable progress we've made as a society over the past decade in dismantling gender norms, but they are, well, the norm. Old habits die hard and even the wokest of the woke can still be shocked by public or private behavior that bucks gendered expectations. Still, Dwayne Johnson breaks these stereotypes so often that it's starting to feel more routine—in a good way.

The American action star may be the ultimate avatar of masculinity but it warrants noting that the men who embody those characters on-screen are often expected to perform masculinity offscreen as well. Sylvester Stallone's star didn't rise because he talked about his struggles with depression in interviews and Instagram captions. Kiefer Sutherland didn't capture our hearts by posting loving, tender pictures of his young daughters to his MySpace page. This certainly isn't to say that these men willingly ascribe to a rigid, structured lifestyle of masculinity or that they're devoid of warmth. It's simply that masculinity is a prison, one that has its snares sunk as deeply in your dad or brother as it does in celebrities and public figures.

In fact, there's an irony in the fact that The Rock became famous through professional wrestling, an industry that even today enforces gender norms more aggressively than almost any other American institution. He first made his name as one of the all-time great trash-talkers in the sport and, in doing so, utilized a dictionary's worth of grossly gendered put-downs several times a week on national television. Insults in pro wrestling almost always are increasingly creative (and increasingly ridiculous) ways of saying, "You're not as manly as I am." Jokes about genitalia, women's underwear, and running home crying to your mommy are the norm. The word *bitch* is thrown around liberally. Pro wrestling is a cacophonous symphony of political incorrectness, and back in the nineties, The Rock was its Mozart.

But though the barrier between character and performer is intentionally thin in pro wrestling, Dwayne Johnson has never been The Rock, even if The Rock has always been Dwayne Johnson. The Rock dished out gendered smack talk like a lunch lady trying to get rid of the mystery meat before it went bad, but that doesn't mean Dwayne Johnson wasn't an open-minded guy circa 2001. And even if he *wasn't*, people grow and change, and Johnson seems to have made the most of his chance to do so over the past twenty years.

Johnson's performance of masculinity is a balancing act of acrobatic proportions. Look at him. The Rock looks like he was carved from granite. He's got one of the most astounding and recognizable physiques in the world, and his Instagram feed is full of gym videos. The fitness gear in his signature Under Armour line is plastered with aggressive slogans like PROGRESS THROUGH PAIN and CHASE GREATNESS. Around the world, gyms have murals of him painted on their walls, a totem of masculine idealization gazing out on clients with a watchful eye, reminding them to, in Johnson's own words, "FOCUS!"

The acting roles he takes often fill surface-level archetypes of masculinity. Soldiers, field agents, and jungle adventurers populate his filmography, the sort of jobs we associate with tough guys. He regularly graces the covers of men's magazines like *GQ* and *Muscle & Fitness*, almost always along with a proclamation of his position: "the fittest man in the world" or "man of the year."

Johnson is seen as embodying everything a modern man should be—but how he sets this standard doesn't begin and end with the size of his biceps.

Counting Calories

The Rock loves cookies, specifically giant chocolate chip cookies with peanut butter spread on top. He loves sushi, pizza, and pancakes as well. We know this because once or twice a week, The Rock posts a picture of a truly epic cheat meal on Instagram, often accompanied by a discussion of whatever documentary or stand-up special he's watching on his night off. Sure, he's got a penchant for true crime, but you're far more likely to see him talking up the latest music documentary to be added to Netflix. He's also talked about watching the heartwarming *Won't You Be My Neighbor?*—twice.

Back to the cookies for a second. How regularly do you see a fitness icon not only talk about but also show off the junk food they eat? Unhealthy idealizations of body type are common in media and largely target women, but an entire industry is built on profiting off the idea that all men can realistically attain the body of actors starring in superhero movies. By sharing photos of his cheat meals, The Rock bucks the notion that fitness is an all-work no-play game. The ethos behind doing this is spelled out in the captions attached to these posts: earn your cheat meals but remember to *enjoy* your cheat meals.

The language with which The Rock discusses fitness is crucial, too. "Hittin' that fatigue zone with 3 hours sleep and pushin' thru this lil' Xmas workout," he captioned a Christmas Day workout post. "But Dwanta must push on . . . " You'll never see Johnson talk about exercise in terms that make getting in shape seem intimidating or unattainable. (True, he regularly works out past midnight, but with a schedule like his, it's implicit that he doesn't expect the same of everyone.) He's intense, sure, but never condescending. Crucially, he rarely talks about fitness as a goal-driven activity but, rather, as a lifestyle decision. He often admits that, beyond being a necessity for shooting movies, his gym time is his "me time." Getting to the gym? That's the entirety of the goal. To Johnson, if you're hitting the gym and making the most of your time there, you're doing plenty. You're earning that cheat meal.

Age Ain't Just a Number

Johnny Depp was forty-six when he starred opposite twenty-three-year-old Amber Heard in *The Rum Diary*. Bruce Willis was nearly fifty when he locked lips with twenty-something Jessica Alba in *Sin City*. The list goes on. Pick any massive, middle-aged male movie star and you're likely to find at least a couple of films in which his love interest is young enough to be his daughter. The exception? You have three guesses and the first two don't count.

Dwayne Johnson's on-screen love interests are almost always around his age. Think of *Skyscraper*'s Neve Campbell and *San Andreas*'s Carla Gugino. You're not likely to see him cast opposite a woman who could be an undergrad unless she's playing his daughter. The notable exception is Karen Gillan in *Jumanji: Welcome to the Jungle*, though by the film's internal logic the characters they play are the same age (Johnson and Gillan play video game avatars controlled by high school students). However, they're never all that intimate on-screen—the physical romantic catharsis is saved for the teenage characters whose avatars they portray.

Although The Rock doesn't write and direct the films he stars in, he's incredibly hands-on as a producer; most films he stars in are at least coproduced by his production company, Seven Bucks. He might not hold the power of his blockbuster cinema contemporary Tom Cruise—who demands approval of the final cut of any film he's in, which infamously made the production and post-production of 2008's *Valkyrie* nightmarish for his editor—but The Rock chooses his projects carefully and has a hand in selecting his costars, approving the script, and everything in between. As such, this pattern of age-appropriate love interests feels like a decision rather than an accident.

Let's Talk about Sex, Baby

Speaking of love interests, let's talk about how women in The Rock's films are rarely objectified. The Rock's films exhibit a peculiar (for Hollywood) lack of male gaze, which can border on total asexuality. For someone who is literally a former recipient of *People* magazine's Sexiest Man Alive award, Johnson seems remarkably unconcerned with making sex a driving factor in his projects. His *Fast & Furious* character Luke Hobbs—his most famous and most revisited role—is revealed to be a father in *Furious 7*, but as of this book's publication we've yet to see a wife or any semblance of a love interest.

The women who star opposite Johnson exist as his equals and are treated with utmost respect by his characters, the camera, and the script. The crux of *Skyscraper* is a *Die Hard*–esque narrative about a man (Will Sawyer) who has to save his family from a gang of bad dudes. It'd be easy for his wife (and two kids) to become a glorified MacGuffin in a story like this, a damsel in distress who spends the film's run time at the mercy of her captors. Instead, Sarah Sawyer is a fully realized character with agency. She makes decisions. She's never objectified by the camera or the characters. Honestly, she *kicks ass*.

Jumanji: Welcome to the Jungle presents another interesting case. Ruby Roundhouse, the badass Lara Croft–esque caricature that the audience sees for much of the film playing opposite The Rock's Dr. Smolder Bravestone, is a stand-in for a teenage girl named Martha. Similarly, The Rock isn't actually playing a ripped, charismatic adventurer but a nerdy kid named Spencer. Ruby's visage not only serves as a meta commentary on overly sexualized women in video games but also functions as a love letter to how badass those characters can be. She does, after all, drop-kick a dude after leaping from a moving motorcycle.

Crucially, Bravestone and Roundhouse aren't the ones who end up together—Spencer and Martha are. The avatars share a hilariously awkward smooch in the game (both confirm that it's their first kiss), but the real romantic catharsis comes after the teens have escaped the game and are back in their real bodies.

Is it sad that treating women like people and not sex objects to be won by protagonists is a notable accomplishment? Absolutely. And let's be clear: the deemphasis on sexuality by The Rock's characters and films does not make them morally superior to others. On-screen sexuality is not inherently problematic. What *is* problematic is how often film portrayals of masculinity are inexorably tied up with the business of sex. The prevailing attitude is that a character can't "be a man" if there isn't a woman in need of rescue and/or seduction. The Rock actively bucks that toxic stereotype by playing characters whose sense of masculinity isn't reliant on ogling women or sweeping them off their feet.

Ladies' Man

Humanizing portrayals of women in The Rock's films is not surprising given that he's publicly self-identified as a feminist, notably in a lengthy 2017 interview with *GQ*, and he's spoken often about the influence women have had on his life. His father, pro wrestler Rocky Johnson, spent much of Dwayne's childhood on the road, leaving Johnson's mother to effectively raise him alone. Now he is a father to three daughters. His ex-wife Dany Garcia remains a close friend and his primary business partner at Seven Bucks Productions. Meanwhile, Johnson has been with his girlfriend, Lauren Hashian, for more than ten years.

The Rock is vocal about the ways being a father to daughters and having been raised by a strong single mother have shaped him. The language he uses when discussing these experiences is far more sentimental than we're used to hearing from men in the public eye. There's a vulnerability and a palpable warmth to the way he talks about them. Pretense and formality are stripped away. "She can be anything she wants," he once wrote in an Instagram post about his middle daughter, Jasmine Lia. "She can sit at any table. She can trailblaze a path, while humbly and gratefully recognizing those before her who paved the way . . ."

The Rock's social media profiles are chock-full of photos of him performing parental duties, including ones that are often thought of as more maternal. The Rock is a regular diaper changer and lullaby singer, and he is no stranger to having a three-year-old paint his nails. Is he entirely unique among fathers in this respect? Not at all. But he's completely unafraid to show off these parts of himself that clash with the very masculine norms one would expect him to uphold.

It's Okay Not to Be Okay

Ranking the most harmful facets of toxic masculinity is futile considering that they're all crappy in their own special way. That being said, the idea that men should not—nay, *cannot*—talk about their feelings is among the most damaging. It is important and healthy to talk about what's going on inside your head and heart. Unfortunately, this dialogue is rarely encouraged among men and boys. The Rock has, in his own way, attempted to destigmatize that conversation.

This is another instance of a little bit going a long way. Though he hasn't established a mental-health nonprofit or appeared as a keynote speaker at an industry convention, The Rock has been open in recent years about his struggles with depression, notably in a widely circulated 2018 Instagram post. He has described the experience of watching his mother try to end her life when he was only fifteen. Years later, after being cut from the Canadian Football League, he struggled with his own low point, not wanting to leave his bedroom and crying constantly. He has acknowledged that, had he not sought help, he might have attempted suicide. This kind of public disclosure can be hard to read at times, but that's the point. It wouldn't be as significant if The Rock were having easy discussions about mental health struggles.

The Rock says that the keys to staying afloat through struggles are simple: empathy and openness. In April 2018 he told the British newspaper *Express*, "We've always got to do our best to pay attention when other people are in pain." Johnson later elaborated on Twitter: "Took me a long time to realize it but the key is to not be afraid to open up. Especially us dudes have a tendency to keep it in. You're not alone."

That statement, short and simple as it might be, speaks volumes. The Rock is fully aware of the position he holds in our culture, of the expectations and responsibilities that come with being one of the most widely loved and recognized male stars in the world. He knows exactly how many millions of Twitter and Instagram followers he has. His words hold value, and he has used that privilege to initiate a difficult conversation, one that men around the world need to have with themselves and their loved ones. It's the last thing you'd expect from a billion-dollar superstar, but, then again, The Rock defying expectations has become the norm.

In the age of #MeToo and #TimesUp, the most we can hope of male icons is that they don't completely and irrevocably screw everything up. It's sad that expectations are so low, but let's be real: we've been conditioned to expect the bare minimum. The Rock didn't rise to fame by dismantling the patriarchy. He doesn't *have* to do any of this. He's got a great smile, and he's buff as hell, and it's fun to watch him fight stuff on big movie screens. He could happily coast into retirement without giving fans anything more than blockbuster entertainment.

But he doesn't. He uses his position of influence to chip away at the toxicity that comes with overt displays of masculinity. These words and actions hold even more meaning coming from a man who has been built up as the platonic ideal of a man. The Rock's approach not only colors our current perspectives on masculinity but, in the long run, will also force stars who come after him to be held to a higher standard. If there's one thing The Rock has taught us, it's that we deserve no less.

THE ROCKSCARS™

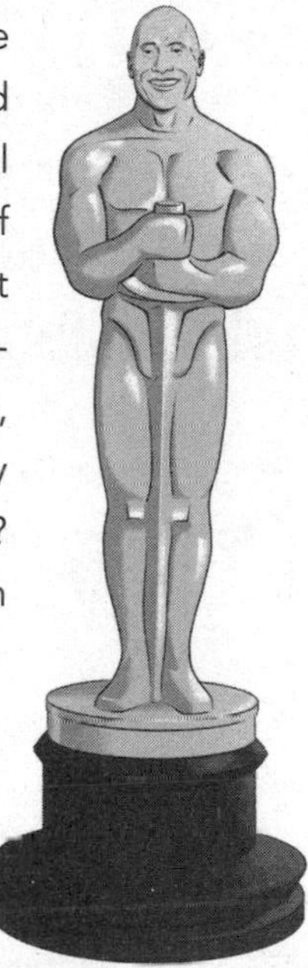

As of the writing of this book, Dwayne "The Rock" Johnson has not received an Academy Award. Is this, in an ethical sense, right? Do the cosmic scales of karma not demand that he have at least three: for *Pain & Gain* (Best Actor in a Supporting Role), *Moana* (Best Original Song), and *Fast Five* (the widely coveted Ricky Bobby Oscar for Best Movie Ever Made)? The slight oversight is that we live in an unjust world, and this is as good a testament to that grim reality as anything.

Why not take the reins of fate into our own hands? Why wait for some faceless organization to dub our hero worthy when we are fully capable of doing so ourselves? On this principle, we gather here today for the inaugural Academy of Motion Picture Arts and Sciences Starring Dwayne "The Rock" Johnson Awards, henceforth to be known as the Rockscars.

The categories, which are profiled below, feature a pool of three to five nominees; a winner will be declared and a brief explanation provided. These results have been determined by science and cannot be disputed unless a movie featuring Dwayne "The Rock" Johnson is released after publication that warrants reconsideration.

BEST COSTAR

Kevin Hart (*Central Intelligence, Jumanji: Welcome to the Jungle*)
Vin Diesel (*Fast & Furious* franchise)
Rob Corddry (*Ballers*)
Jason Statham (*Furious 7; The Fate of the Furious*)

And the Rockscar goes to . . . Vin Diesel in *Fast & Furious*
Yes, there's beef. Yes, their time as costars in the *Fast & Furious* franchise may have already ended, burning out too soon like a comet in the night sky. But no other pairing can match the electric chemistry of these two. That first time they face off in *Fast Five*? The knock-down drag-out brawl that follows? That epic scene in which Dom pulls Hobbs from the ground after the assault from the drug dealers? All of those moments are legendary. Yeah, it's fun to watch The Rock quip back and forth with Kevin Hart but let's be real: Johnson is at his best when playing opposite Diesel.

BEST QUOTE

"You're like a black Will Smith." (*Central Intelligence*)

ROMAN: "Better hide your baby oil."
HOBBS: "Better hide that big-ass forehead."
(*Fast & Furious 6*)

"I will beat you like a Cherokee drum." (*The Fate of the Furious*)

"Jesus Christ himself blessed me with many gifts! One of them is knocking someone the f*** out!" (*Pain & Gain*)

"Daddy's gotta go to work." (*Furious 7*)

And the Rockscar goes to . . . *Pain & Gain*

Pain & Gain is a surreal fever dream of a movie full of quotable bits, but no moment captures its utter madness quite like when The Rock's Paul Doyle punches Tony Shalhoub's Victor in the face and exclaims in agony, "Jesus Christ himself has blessed me with many gifts! One of them is knocking someone the f*** out!" The cherry on top is the Team Jesus tee he's wearing while saying it. It's such a singularly bizarre moment that it can't not win this prize.

FUNNIEST PERFORMANCE

Pain & Gain

Central Intelligence

Jumanji: Welcome to the Jungle

Moana

And the Rockscar goes to . . . *Pain & Gain*

Both *Central Intelligence* and *Jumanji* give us versions of The Rock in which he's playing against type in endearing fashion. They're both hysterical performances for sure. But *Pain & Gain* shows The Rock on another level, viciously blasting modern American masculinity to hell with the explosiveness of a bundle of dynamite. In *Pain & Gain*,

The Rock is funnier, weirder, and more memorable than he's ever been.

BEST FIGHT SCENE THAT ISN'T HOBBS VS. DOM IN *FAST FIVE* BECAUSE THAT'D BE TOO OBVIOUS

Roadblock vs. Firefly (*G. I. Joe: Retaliation*)
Hobbs vs. Shaw (*Furious 7*)
Davis and George the Giant Gorilla vs. giant monsters (*Rampage*)

And the Rockscar goes to . . . Hobbs vs. Shaw in *Furious 7*
The fight that launched a spinoff film. Yes, their on-screen banter in the franchise's eighth installment is ultimately what made audiences realize they needed a Hobbs–Shaw team-up movie, but that banter wouldn't be possible without the foundation of their badass throw-down in the prior film. What a way to open a movie, huh? These two dudes go through a glass table, and the fight ends only because Hobbs throws himself out a window onto a car to save his partner's life. It is an absolute banger in every sense of the word.

BEST ROMANTIC PAIRING

Neve Campbell (Sarah Sawyer, *Skyscraper*)
Karen Gillan (Ruby Roundhouse, *Jumanji: Welcome to the Jungle*)
Melissa McCarthy (Darla McGuckian, *Central Intelligence*)

And the Rockscar goes to . . . Melissa McCarthy in *Central Intelligence*

Melissa McCarthy appears in *Central Intelligence* for all of two and a half minutes. In that time, her character is reunited with The Rock's Bob Stone after they have spent decades apart. While Stone stands naked in front of their entire high-school reunion, Darla reveals that she has not one but two lazy eyes, and she performs the ultimate The Rock love interest wish-fulfillment task: feeling his pecs. Hilarity aside, the two have a really sweet chemistry for those few minutes, far more than you're likely to see in almost any serious on-screen pairing in a summer blockbuster. It's just one of the many ways in which *Central Intelligence* succeeds far more than it needs to.

GREATEST FEAT OF STRENGTH

Executing the Leap (*Skyscraper*)
Flexing out of a full-arm cast (*Furious 7*)
Doing bicep curls with a concrete desk
(*The Fate of the Furious*)
Beating John Cena (WrestleMania XXVIII)

And the Rockscar goes to . . . flexing out of a full-arm cast in *Furious 7*

If you have not yet seen the moment in *Furious 7* in which Hobbs tells his young daughter, "Daddy's gotta go to work," and then flexes his arm so hard that the plaster cast encasing it cracks into pieces, your life is emptier than you realize.

BEST PERFORMANCE BY DWAYNE "THE ROCK" JOHNSON IN A MOVIE FEATURING DWAYNE "THE ROCK" JOHNSON

Dwayne "The Rock" Johnson as Bob Stone (*Central Intelligence*)
Dwayne "The Rock" Johnson as Luke Hobbs
(*Fast & Furious* franchise)
Dwayne "The Rock" Johnson as Maui (*Moana*)
Dwayne "The Rock" Johnson as Paul Doyle (*Pain & Gain*)

And the Rockscar goes to . . . Dwayne "The Rock" Johnson as Luke Hobbs in *Fast & Furious* franchise

Are you surprised? Who else could take this one? The Rock does the best acting of his career in *Pain & Gain* and proves himself a true renaissance man in *Moana*, but let's be honest: there is no character who better captures what's great about The Rock than Luke Hobbs, the baddest DSS agent on the planet. He drops dope one-liners and knocks out bad guys like Tyson in his prime. And he does so only after having made sure his daughter's soccer team is set to clinch a win. Hobbs is everything great about The Rock rolled into one little—okay, noticeably not so little—package.

BEST MOVIE STARRING DWAYNE "THE ROCK" JOHNSON

Moana
Pain & Gain
Central Intelligence
G. I. Joe: Retaliation
Fast Five

And the Rockscar goes to . . . *Fast Five*

In the interest of fairness, let's first hear the case for the rest of our nominees.

Though its overall objective quality is up for debate, not enough love is given to *G. I. Joe: Retaliation.* As Bill Hader's beloved *Saturday Night Live* character Stefon might say, this movie has *everything*: explosions, Bruce Willis, a chase scene across a mountainside with ninjas, *RZA playing an old-school blind kung-fu master.* It's a big, dumb, loud action movie of the best sort, and The Rock is in fine form throughout.

Moana is a perfect movie. It's full of heart and wonderful music and excellent vocal performances. Maui belting out his signature song "You're Welcome" is an all-time great The Rock moment. It's also one of the rare good Rock movies you can watch with children without subjecting them to violence and/or sex jokes.

Pain & Gain features the best Rock performance but does so by taking a pessimistic stance on the sort of characters Johnson often plays. It's good, but it's not necessarily what you want from a Rock movie in that it kind of sets out to make you feel bad about enjoying The Rock's movies.

There's no more pleasantly surprising The Rock movie than *Central Intelligence.* What comes off in trailers as an exhausting, derivative buddy comedy is instead a delightful, inventive flick that features both lead actors (The Rock and Kevin Hart) successfully playing against type. The plot twists are as shocking as anything Christopher Nolan has written, and the jokes are as killer as those in any Judd Apatow comedy. *Central Intelligence* is a gem long overdue for a cultural reevaluation, a veritable cult classic in the making.

However, there can be only one winner and we have come to a single, indisputable conclusion: *Fast Five* is the best Dwayne "The Rock" Johnson movie. Are you surprised? Of course you aren't. This is the easiest call since The Rock turned down the *Tooth Fairy* sequel (shout-out to Larry the Cable Guy for filling in). It introduces us to his most iconic character, Diplomatic Security Service Agent Luke Hobbs. Vin Diesel and The Rock have a brawl for the ages. The Rock has a goatee and it looks good. The pacing, the photography, the action choreography—it's all top-notch. *Fast Five* is action cinema running on all four cylinders. It might be the best movie ever made. It's everything you'd want from a Dwayne "The Rock" Johnson movie.

WORST DWAYNE "THE ROCK" JOHNSON MOVIE

Tooth Fairy

And the Rockscar goes to . . . *Tooth Fairy*

This movie is a federal crime. There will be no elaboration.

REMEDIAL (ROCKMEDIAL?) MULTIVERSE THEORY

A Brief Look at Characters The Rock Has Almost Played

Today the idea that a project with Dwayne "The Rock" Johnson attached might *not* go into production and make a hundred million dollars is unheard of. Isn't greenlighting a movie he's game to star in like printing money for production studios? Unfortunately, Hollywood can be a fickle beast, and even a career as spectacular as The Rock's is speckled with a few notable almosts and near hits. Somewhere in the vast expanse of the multiverse there lies a timeline in which The Rock took on a few notable roles that fell through in our reality. We might never know what some of these films would have looked like. Luckily, the world of imagination isn't bound by the confines of reality.

The following is a list of characters that were very nearly played by The Rock. Some could happen in the future; the door has closed on others. Either way, it's fascinating to imagine what these performances might have looked like had fate cast a kinder eye upon them.

Willy Wonka

For a not-insignificant portion of visionary director Tim Burton's career, he seemed to assume that a Constitutional amendment required him to cast Johnny Depp in the starring role of every movie he made. From 2005 to 2012 the two collaborated consecutively on *Charlie and the Chocolate Factory, Corpse Bride, Sweeney Todd, Alice in Wonderland,* and *Dark Shadows*, and prior to that streak they collaborated on three other films. For a time their partnership seemed like one of life's few certainties, up there with death, taxes, and the eventual heat-death of the universe. It's mind-blowing, then, to learn that the first of their five-film collaborative streak almost didn't happen.

Despite his track record, Tim Burton does consider other actors for roles before eventually handing them to Depp. In fact, there seems to be no role he cast with more indecision than that of Willy Wonka in his adaptation of Roald Dahl's *Charlie and the Chocolate Factory*. Just a few of the actors considered (listed in ascending order of weirdness): Will Smith, Brad Pitt, Christopher Walken, Robin Williams, Jim Carrey, Robert De Niro, Nicolas Cage, and *Marilyn freakin' Manson* (who probably would have delivered the exact same performance Depp gave, but with more latex). And none of those folks were Burton's first choice! His initial pick for the role was, of all people, The Rock.

This fact is a little less surprising when you remember that the film was slated for a 2005 release, right around the time The Rock was beginning to transition from pure action movies to a more diverse and often family-friendly filmography. Ringing in this era by stepping in as an already-beloved character would have made sense. Burton's original choice also is easier to picture when you consider how the film is built around Depp's bizarre, eccentric take on Willy Wonka. Burton is no rookie director; had The Rock been cast, it's likely the film would have been tailored to accommodate his performance.

That said, who's to say The Rock's performance wouldn't have been just as zany? If films like *Central Intelligence* and *Southland Tales* have taught us anything, it's that not only is The Rock not afraid to get weird, he's also good at it. Imagine your favorite of his zanier performances and then look at it through Burton's trademark kaleidoscope of madness. Better yet, imagine buff Willy Wonka. We were robbed of buff Willy Wonka.

Lobo

Are we *really* living in the golden age of comic book movies if The Rock hasn't played a superhero? Marvel and DC have made so many superhero movies over the past twenty years that when an actor as esteemed as Jude Law finally got on board, he was cast as Yon-Rogg. Nobody can tell you who Yon-Rogg is without hitting up Wikipedia. We're in obscure territory here, but somehow we've yet to see The Rock play a comic book superhero.

To be fair, he was cast as villain/antihero Black Adam in the DC Extended Universe, but as of this book's publication he has yet to appear as that character. Rumored appearances include a Black Adam solo film and the sequel to April 2019's *Shazam!* (Black Adam is the longtime rival/

nemesis of the titular superhero). But until the first camera starts rolling, all that is up in the air. If fans looking forward to *Man of Steel 2* or Marvel's long-promised *Inhumans* movie have learned anything, it's that plans are always subject to change. Fans of The Rock have even more reason to be skeptical because this is not the first time he's been attached to a big role in a superhero movie.

A DC comic book character, Lobo is an intergalactic alien bounty hunter who looks kind of like the Crow if the Crow was your friend's greasy stepdad who spends all day working on his Harley. He's crass as hell, sort of a proto-Deadpool for comic fans in the eighties. Lobo isn't quite the household name that Superman and Batman are, but he's got a passionate fan base that has long yearned for him to take the box office by storm.

For years it was rumored that were Lobo to hit the big screen, he'd be played by The Rock, an ideal casting choice. The stars finally seemed to align on July 15, 2012, when The Rock responded to a fan inquiry about the Lobo buzz by saying, "Rumors of me possibly playing Lobo are true. Joel Silver and Brad Peyton [future *San Andreas* and *Rampage* director] are working on it now. That could be fun."

Less than a year later the project was dead. The Rock confirmed in a February 2013 interview with MTV that "it just kind of went away." Since then, the character's big-screen train has come to a halt. Lobo made an appearance on season 2 of the SyFy show *Krypton*, just not performed by The Rock. Black Adam will likely go over better with casual moviegoers than Lobo would have, but it's still fun to imagine The Rock playing a bulky black-and-white alien biker maniac.

Johnny Bravo

Imagine The Rock in his pajamas, bowl of cereal in hand, perched in front of his TV on a Saturday morning. Maybe he's lying on the couch or sitting on the floor. You can imagine a cute pair of slippers if you'd like. There are classic Saturday morning cartoons on the screen.

That exercise probably put a smile on your face. Here's some good news: there's at least *some* truth to it. The Rock is a big ol' fanboy of a great many things—notably Elvis Presley (most of the Elvis memorabilia his character owns in *The Game Plan* is from The Rock's real-life collection) and cartoons. Or at least one cartoon in particular.

Johnny Bravo aired on Cartoon Network from 1997 to 2004. The titular character was a self-styled wannabe ladies' man who got into shenanigans every week that were almost always tied to trying to woo a different woman. Today, a show about a guy who relentlessly bugs women to date him would be a PR nightmare; Johnny's romantic efforts are never rewarded—he's a bozo for sure—but the show paints him as more lovable than it should. At the time, however, it was a huge hit and a cornerstone program of the network's primetime Cartoon Cartoon Fridays block. The show regularly pulled in great ratings and at one point even had a line of fast-food toys.

The Rock was one of the show's biggest fans, which makes sense; a goofy wannabe Casanova who styles himself like Elvis is right up The Rock's alley. In 2002, around the time The Rock was breaking into Hollywood, Warner Bros. was looking to produce a live-action take on the character. After The Rock mentioned to producers Neal Moritz and Marty Adelstein that he was a huge fan of the show, they aggressively pushed for the film to be greenlit, with him attached.

In this particular case nothing was all that official. Projects in Hollywood are never a sure thing. Having missed his shot at cinematic immortality, Johnny lives on in the form of reruns and the frat bro at the bar who won't stop hitting on that girl who's made it very clear she isn't interested.

Jack Burton

Suggest to a movie buff that a single one of acclaimed genre director John Carpenter's classics should ever be remade and you're likely to get your ass kicked. Carpenter created the horror genre as we know it with the original *Halloween* in 1978 and also gave us *The Fog, Escape from New York, The Thing,* and *They Live*, among others.

One of the odder films from the golden era of Carpenter is *Big Trouble in Little China*, a 1986 action film starring Kurt Russell as Jack Burton, a rough-and-tumble trucker who gets caught up in a mythical battle between ancient beings in Los Angeles's Chinatown, with the fate of the world at stake. It's exactly as unusual as it sounds, which is probably why, despite bombing at the box office, it later developed a die-hard cult following. Russell does *the absolute most* as Burton, hamming it up at every conceivable turn. There's a sorcerer and an ancient curse and kung-fu ninjas.

Nothing a filmmaker could do would improve the film, but we live in an age of reboots and remakes. A studio was bound to come for *Big Trouble in Little China* eventually, and if you're going to reboot a cult classic starring a beloved actor in a once-in-a-lifetime performance, you might as well go big. And you can't go much bigger than The Rock.

Rumors of a sequel have circulated since the release of the original. Carpenter planned the story for a follow-up early on (it was eventually adapted as a comic series by Eric Powell and Brian Churilla for Boom! Studios), but for decades it remained stuck in development hell. Finally, in 2015 news broke that Twentieth Century Fox was developing a remake that would be produced by and star The Rock.

For three years all was quiet. Then in 2018 Hiram Garcia, president of production at Seven Bucks, confirmed that the project was still in development, albeit with a key change. "You can't remake a classic like that, so what we're planning to do is we're gonna continue the story," Garcia said in an August 2018 interview with *Collider*. Don't call it a comeback, Burton's been here for years.

Since that announcement, The Rock has been swamped with multiple projects and there have been no further developments. Seeing The Rock hamming it up as the simultaneously bumbling and badass Jack Burton would make for a great Saturday night at the movies, not to mention it'd be closer to reality than either Lobo or Willy Wonka. But given this project's long, troubled road to production, this is a movie you'd best not believe before you see it.

Doc Savage

Outside of the *Fast & Furious* franchise, The Rock has not yet worked with any of the great film directors of our time. It's fun to imagine what he could do under the guidance of someone like Steven Soderbergh, Guillermo del Toro, or Christopher Nolan. For a brief time in 2016 it seemed like we might get a glimpse of such a pairing.

Shane Black is one of the more iconoclastic auteurs in modern Hollywood. After writing the script for *Lethal Weapon* he penned a number of beloved action flicks before venturing into the world of directing. His films *Kiss Kiss Bang Bang* and *The Nice Guys* are riotous comedy-crime romps that riff on life in Hollywood and the detective archetypes developed in pulp novels. Between his uniquely modern sensibilities and adoration for the pulps, the 2009 announcement that he would bring Doc Savage into the twenty-first century came as no surprise.

Doc Savage is an icon of the pulps whom Marvel mastermind Stan Lee credited as being the precursor to modern superheroes. He's part Indiana Jones and part Batman, having trained his body to master the martial arts and his mind to develop a photographic memory. An archaeologist, an explorer, and a detective, his job description alone could fill its own novel. Ultimately, Savage is an adventurer. Does that sound like the perfect role for The Rock? Black thought so as well.

In 2016, hot on the heels of *The Nice Guys*, Black and The Rock agree to team up on a Doc Savage movie. But soon Black was tapped to make Fox's long-awaited *Predator* sequel *The Predator*, and in the following years both men stayed busy, albeit never on the same film.

During the promotional tour for 2018's *Rampage*, The Rock noted that the project wasn't dead but indefinitely on hold. "That project had a few issues, not creative issues but more so business affairs issues . . . we're still kind of working through," he told *Collider*. He added that, "whether it's that project or something else, we've [Shane and I] made a pact that we're going to work together at some point in our careers." With both men booked up for the foreseeable future, it might be a while before we see what their collaboration will look like and if it will involve the beloved pulp hero. Either way, if someone plans on making a Doc Savage movie anytime soon, they'd best keep The Rock in mind. He's clearly the man for the job.

PART III

The Rock and His Fans

Think back to long ago, to a time before constant information overload and the twenty-four-hour meme cycle. Go all the way back, possibly as many as ten years ago, to the first time you logged on to Twitter and realized that you could tweet at your favorite celebrity—sing their praises unprompted, respond to an open query they posted, whatever struck your fancy. Though it was far from guaranteed, there was at least a chance that *they might tweet back*. A great deal has been said and written about the ways that social media has reshaped the very concepts of communication and celebrity in the modern era. But if you're of a certain generation, your conception of social media is likely, and largely, shaped by that first tweet you sent to your favorite celebrity.

Twitter, which launched in March 2006, is far from the first or only social network to facilitate the connection between public figures and their fans (or haters). Before there was Twitter, MySpace (cue PTSD flashbacks for an entire generation of scene kids) allowed up-and-coming bands to share their music to a wider audience than ever before and interact with their fans through blog posts. This, like Twitter, was revolutionary. No longer was the release and promotion of music dependent on the whimsy of capricious agents and record label managers. Suddenly, a new band could record an EP and not have to worry about signing with a label, or even investing in a CD run. They could just share it on their MySpace page and engage directly with their audience. This fact pushed the music industry into the digital era while removing barriers between artists and their fans.

Thanks to apps like Instagram and Twitter, today your favorite actors, musicians, and athletes are more accessible than they've ever been. Yet not all of them take advantage of this. Many celebrities use social media simply to facilitate the illusion of accessibility. All due respect to LeBron James, but his Twitter feed is pretty much devoid of interaction with his fans.

And that's fine! LeBron is one of the greatest basketball players of all time, still in his prime, and he has myriad professional responsibilities outside of basketball, as well as a family, to take care of. He's under zero obligation to send thank-you DMs to fans or address their barrage of tweets about that triple-double that Steph Curry hit the other night.

That he posts his casual thoughts on basketball, pop culture, and the world around him already makes him far more open and accessible to fans than Michael Jordan ever was.

LeBron is just one example. You could insert the name of any high-profile celebrity and there's a fair chance that they're more Mariah Carey than Chrissy Teigen when it comes to social media. Nobody is obligated to respond to tweets or Instagram comments, least of all someone who is touring the world or filming a movie.

That's what makes The Rock significant: at any given moment there's a good chance he's doing one of those two things. He takes little to no time off between projects and sets out on massive worldwide press tours when a film launches. He's got a family, a busy production company, a clothing line, and every other ostensible business venture under the sun. His reputation as the hardest working man in showbiz is no exaggeration, which makes it even more impressive that he takes every opportunity to connect with his fans.

On social media, The Rock seems to be in a perpetual state of engagement with his massive fan base, which at the time of this writing clocks in at more than 13 million on Twitter and over 150 million on Instagram. He posts daily, sharing everything from workout snapshots to cheat meal photos to quiet moments with his family, friends, and coworkers. On Instagram you'll almost never see a photo without an extensive caption; The Rock isn't one for posting half of a Drake quote or a couple of emojis. Instead he writes lengthy messages singing the praises of whoever is in the photograph with him, waxing poetic on his state of mind during his workout or singing the praises of the costars on the project he's filming. Sometimes he just talks about how much he loves Johnny Cash.

Being a celebrity means that literally anything you post on the internet is going to receive dozens, hundreds, or even thousands of comments, a good sixty percent of which will have absolutely nothing to do with the original post. The Rock? He responds to them earnestly. He answers questions, wishes people happy birthday, and playfully ribs haters. He doesn't respond to every single comment, because how could he? There's always a mountain of them to go through. That he takes a few minutes to engage with his fans personally is more effort than most put in.

And make no mistake, many of these comments are quite personal. Commenters routinely share long accounts about internal struggles, fitness journeys, and battles through disease, homelessness, and countless other grim experiences. It seems that because he is perpetually open on social media, fans feel comfortable sharing their stories with him. They're not forcing a dialogue with him but, rather, being as forthcoming and vulnerable as he is.

The emotional labor of engaging with a stranger's heartfelt personal anecdote is a burden that The Rock is not obligated to take on. That he's a central figure in so many of these stories, despite never having met most of the people telling them, is a heavy responsibility for anyone to bear. But it's a responsibility he doesn't seem to take lightly. The Rock shares words of praise and encouragement that surely offer a kind of closure or peace.

The Rock can't fix our problems. But he seems to recognize that offering a simple comment like "I'm proud of you" takes little effort but goes a long way.

Take another look at The Rock's Instagram feed and you'll find an astounding number of pictures of him rocking a big cornball smile and standing next to people he's meeting for the first time. These people aren't network executives, costars, or new personal trainers. No, they're fans. And often he is the one wearing the biggest smile.

The Rock also dedicates an inordinate amount of time to meeting fans face-to-face. When filming on location, he'll frequently post videos of the lines of fans who wait all day outside the set to meet him, or at least simply get a glimpse at their idol as he leaves for the day. The Rock, of course, takes time to greet each and every one—even if doing so means staying out until the witching hour. Movies often shoot for at *least* twelve hours a day, and it's not uncommon for him to leave set as late as two a.m. It's a testament to his following that fans show up before his day begins and are still there when it ends.

To his credit, The Rock makes the wait worthwhile. Sure, he might play around a little; he has posted videos of him faking out the waiting fans, driving past them with nothing more than a slight wave, but he always comes back to say hi, take a photo, or give an autograph.

Why does he do it? Is it all a grueling PR feat? Couldn't he be doing literally anything else with his time, such as sleeping? (Unrelated, but when does The Rock sleep?) The answer is simple: he knows what it's like to have your heroes disappoint you. Shortly after he began acting, he ran into a fellow actor (who remains unnamed) of whom he'd been a big fan for a long time. At the time The Rock had yet to gain acceptance as an actor, and audiences and Hollywood stars alike still viewed him as a pro wrestler with delusions of grandeur. Rather than extend a helping hand and show The Rock kindness, the actor big-shotted him, barely giving him the time of day.

This experience, which The Rock has discussed in an Instagram post, stuck with him. He swore he'd never make someone else feel the way he felt in that moment. Since then he has spent hours greeting fans, taken selfies from his car window in the middle of traffic, and invited Make-a-Wish recipients to his sets for days that rival anything Willy Wonka could arrange.

The Rock comes from humble beginnings. He's talked at length about his experiences with homelessness, poverty, and being so flat broke that he had to move back in with his parents after being cut from the Canadian Football League in 1995. His circumstances today couldn't be more different. Although his unrivaled work ethic is largely responsible for his successful career, he knows better than anyone that it all goes away without his fans.

Statements like “I wouldn’t be here without my fans” often read as lip service when coming from the mouths of celebrities. It’s the thing they’re expected to say, an obligation between “my family” and “my producers/managers/agent/etc.” Stars who rush past fans gathered outside movie premieres, ignore engagement on social media, and refuse selfies have uttered lines like this one, and their actions dilute any genuine sentiment behind the words.

Who could blame them? To be perceived as “nice,” a public figure has to constantly be on, always ready to interact and live up to the expectations their celebrity has established. It’s hard to blame someone as famous as Jake Gyllenhaal for seeming reluctant to engage with fans who wait for him outside of clubs and restaurants. The constant noise and pressure to perform, lest your reputation be damaged irreparably, is of a crushing magnitude that is difficult to fathom it unless you’ve experienced it firsthand.

No celebrity is inherently bad for not striving to be endlessly approachable. This is a hell of a task to take on, one that often accentuates the contradictions between a public persona and a private life. Certainly, outright rudeness is never acceptable. Decency takes very little effort or time. Howevever, giving of oneself and one’s personal time, as many celebs are expected to do, takes quite a lot.

That’s why the lengths The Rock goes to for his fans mean so much to them. Every tweet, every Instagram reply, and every heartfelt, sincere in-person interaction requires time and energy that he doesn’t *need* to give. That he does foster such special relationships with his fans is a remarkable feat that has fostered a well-earned loyalty between Dwayne "The Rock" Johnson and his millions (AND MILLIONS) of fans around the world.

THE SHAPE OF ROCK TO COME; OR, THE ROAD TO EGOT

The Rock will achieve the EGOT. It is an inevitability. He has won every award from Razzies to Teen Choice Awards. The only honors that have eluded him in fifteen years in Hollywood are the Emmy, Grammy, Oscar, and Tony. There was a time when the idea of him winning even one of these seemed unlikely—let's be honest, critics were hardly making Academy Award predictions after *Faster*. Yet, years later, Johnson is one of the most resonant and enduring figures in all entertainment. If anyone in the current pop cultural landscape is destined to EGOT (yes, it's a verb too), it is The Rock.

First, a primer for those unfamiliar with the term: EGOT is an accomplishment achieved when an artist wins an Emmy, Grammy, Oscar, and Tony. Though the possibility of winning all four awards has existed for decades, the term EGOT was popularized by the *30 Rock* episode "Dealbreakers Talk Show #0001," in which Tracy Morgan's character, Tracy Jordan, discovers a necklace that spells EGOT in diamond-studded letters. Said necklace once belonged to *Miami Vice* star Philip Michael Thomas. Once Jordan discovers what EGOT means, he makes achieving it his career goal. The joke is hilarious—Tracy Jordan is not only *not* an accomplished actor but also a total buffoon—but it's even funnier when you learn that it's not just a bit made for the show. Thomas really coined the term and really wore that necklace. Alas, he has never won any of the four awards.

Fewer than twenty entertainers have managed to EGOT, the most notable of whom are Audrey Hepburn, John Legend, Mel Brooks, and Whoopi Goldberg (yes, Daytime Emmys count). Meryl Streep hasn't EGOTed. Steven Spielberg wishes he could. Most EGOT winners work primarily in music, which is honored by all four awards.

The possibility of the Rock EGOTing wasn't on people's minds until Disney and Pixar's *Moana* was released in 2016. The film features The Rock voicing the Polynesian demigod Maui. His performance reveals that he's got a hell of a set of pipes, which he showcases in "You're Welcome," one of the film's standout songs. As awards season drew near, *Moana* became a frontrunner in both the animated film and original song categories. Suddenly it seemed plausible that in all of the infinite timelines drifting through the multiverse, we might be living in one in which The Rock wins an Oscar and a Grammy in the same year.

A different song from the film, "How Far I'll Go," received the Oscar nomination for best original song, and it lost to

"City of Stars" from *La La Land* (a movie you'd forgotten existed until you read this sentence). Still, what had been put out into the universe could not be erased. The Rock could EGOT. No, one day the Rock *will* EGOT. The only question is . . . how?

Intense study of The Rock's filmography, career trajectory, areas of talent, and the laws of physics indicate a variety of possibilities, some more likely than others. What follows is an analysis of possible ways The Rock could EGOT. Please keep in mind that because these timelines are entirely speculative, if the Rock somehow manages to EGOT for, like, *Space Jam 3* or something, the prophecy has still technically been fulfilled.

Timeline 1

The Rock's show *Ballers* is the third-highest-rated 30-minute HBO program of all time. It's also absolutely not winning an Emmy anytime soon. The show is light and fun, decently written, and endearingly performed by Johnson and the rest of the cast. (Denzel Washington's son John David Washington consistently steals the show.) Ten years ago it might have garnered Emmy nominations alongside *Entourage* and *The New Adventures of Old Christine*. However, the comedy genre has since been elevated by shows like *Atlanta* and *Veep*. *Ballers*, which focuses on the lives of elite athletes who thrive on competition, ironically cannot compete.

Still, Rock gotta EGOT. After the show ends, he doesn't want to surrender his grip on television but also refuses to return unless it's in a role that could position him for an Emmy. When *Big Little Lies* director Jean-Marc Vallée needs someone to step in last minute on his new miniseries to play Rooney Mara's husband (John Slattery is forced to drop out), Johnson takes the job with three weeks' notice, venturing completely outside his comfort zone. The project, titled *Evergreen*, explores the complex marriage between a young woman and a man twenty years her senior. The riveting drama shows viewers a side of Johnson they've never seen before. The on-set shouting matches between him and Vallée become the stuff of legend, but the result is the best acting of his career. It doesn't go unnoticed. Later that year he is awarded the Primetime Emmy for outstanding lead actor in a limited series or movie.

Having tasted recognition for his craft, Johnson dives into headier roles than he's taken on in the past. Previously he had thought there was no adrenaline rush like making his grand entrance as a pro wrestler, but that was before he experienced the split second before the winner of the Emmy was announced. Nothing has ever matched that high.

With an Emmy under his belt he begins his quest for the Big O, as he begins publicly referring to the Oscar. Though he still puts out a solid blockbuster film every spring or summer, his fall and winter fare begin catering more to the awards season crowd. After a couple of duds, including a shockingly disastrous turn as a cancer patient in Marc Webb's *Thrive*, he gains traction as an Oscar contender for the first time in director David O. Russell's satirical dramedy

Follow, a heavily fictionalized retelling of the role Twitter played in the 2016 election. Johnson costars as the caustic and anxiety-ridden bodyguard of the analogue for Twitter founder Jack Dorsey (played by James Franco). The Academy takes the bait. Later that year the trailer for the final *Fast & Furious* film advertises "Academy Award Winner Dwayne 'The Rock' Johnson."

Shortly afterward he knocks out the Grammy and the Tony in one fell swoop. Johnson originates the role of his grandfather, "High Chief" Peter Maivia, in the musical *Squared Circle Dynasty*, a musical retelling of his family's lineage in pro wrestling written by his *Moana* collaborator Lin-Manuel Miranda. The *Hamilton* scribe once again produces the show of the year, and Johnson spends a month on Broadway as well as appearing on the original cast recording. The Grammy for best musical theater album and Tony for best performance by a featured actor in a musical follow in short order. The Rock has joined the Legion of EGOT.

Timeline 2

As cofounder of juggernaut film studio Seven Bucks Productions, The Rock oversees the production of successful films (most of which he stars in). But the studio doesn't make just blockbuster films. It also produces reality TV such as *Wake Up Call* and *The Titan Games* and documentaries, largely focusing on inspirational underdog stories. He also produced and briefly appeared in the jarring 2017 documentary *Rock and a Hard Place*, which chronicles a youth prison boot camp. He's got a clear passion for this sort of material; a peek at his Instagram most Saturday evenings shows photos or videos of him chowing down on a cheat meal (usually pancakes) and watching a documentary (true crime seems to be his favorite genre) on his laptop.

From 2018 on, Seven Bucks continues to produce blockbuster cinema but also makes at least one documentary per year. A few years later they strike gold with *The Champ Is Here*, an eight-part series on HBO chronicling the final year of WWE superstar John Cena's wrestling career. The series is shockingly moving; it shows Cena at his weakest and most physically and emotionally vulnerable, as the longtime industry veteran fights the accelerating deterioration of his body in order to end his career on the high note his fans deserve. Acclaim follows, as does the Primetime Emmy for outstanding documentary or nonfiction series.

For the next few years Dwayne sticks to blockbusters. He finishes out the *Fast & Furious* franchise and appears in a few DC Extended Universe films as the supervillain/antihero Black Adam while churning out original content with Seven Bucks Productions. After his third *Jumanji* film (another smash hit), he shocks the world by retiring from acting at age fifty-five.

However, he doesn't leave the film world entirely. After taking a year off he returns to documentary filmmaking, this time as a director rather than a producer. Having spent years overseeing the production of documentaries, he's a natural. His first feature-length doc is nominated for an Oscar, but it's his second, a tearjerker that follows a high-school football team during the season after a local tragedy, that earns him the Academy Award.

After a string of directorial successes, he shocks the world by returning to acting—albeit not on camera. He's one of the lead voice actors in the Lin-Manuel Miranda directed Pixar feature *Among the Stars*. Miranda and Johnson play two grandfathers who sign up for a yearlong expedition into space. It's a smash hit—shocker, huh?—and features music penned by both men. The film's title track easily snags Johnson another Oscar, as well as the Grammy for best song written for visual media.

With his passion for acting reignited, Johnson decides to take on the one field he's always avoided: theater. After scoping out a number of compelling projects he nearly settles on playing Willy Loman in a Kenneth Lonergan–directed revival of *Death of a Salesman*. However, he drops out after Casey Affleck is cast, citing ethical objections. Still, he has caught the theater bug and the warm reception of his near debut gets him thinking. Rather than find a new play, he writes his own. In a one-man show simply titled *Rock* he combines his trademark charm and storytelling ability to narrate the tale of his life and career. It's entertaining but doesn't shy away from tough moments, and Johnson's vulnerability and candor earn much critical acclaim. It wins the Tony Award for best play and completes the rare awards-show Voltron that is the EGOT. It took him over sixty years, but The Rock has finally gotten his EGOT on.

Timeline 3

The Rock has been up-front about the fact that he does not plan to run for President of the United States of America in the 2020 election. He's not lying. He holds off until 2024 to do so. Serving two back-to-back terms, he's unseen in Hollywood for eight long years. Of course, during that time he does everything in his power to make the world outside Tinseltown a better place. For the most part, he succeeds.

However, as his second term comes to a close in early 2033, and president-elect and fellow HBO alum Cynthia Nixon takes her rightful place in the Oval Office, he finds himself once again hungry for Hollywood, for performance, for acting. But he now worries that a return to action cinema would come off hollow, like a nostalgic cash grab—plus, at sixty years old he lacks the physicality he brought to earlier hits like *Fast Five* and *San Andreas*. A drastic reinvention is necessary.

Luckily, the perfect opportunity for someone who's just held office presents itself. Lin-Manuel Miranda is reviving his generation-defining smash hit *Hamilton*, albeit this time with a twist. In this new imagining the roles are gender swapped; the musical now tells the story of Alexandra Hamilton and her journey to unite a young nation alongside cohorts such as Erin Burr, Georgina Washington, and Jenn Laurens. Still hardly looking a day over forty, The Rock steps in as Eli Schuyler. (Miranda plays the only character whose gender does not change: the smarmy King George.)

The revival proves that, in *Hamilton*'s case, lightning *can* strike twice. It garners a multitude of Tony awards, including best actor in a musical for The Rock.

With Rockymania sweeping the nation once again, acclaimed screenwriter Aaron Sorkin approaches Johnson with the most obvious project possible: a film about the unlikely presidency of a former professional wrestler, Dwayne "The Rock" Johnson. It seems like a vanity project, but then again, Sorkin turned a movie about Facebook into a generation-defining masterpiece. The Rock signs on to play himself in a biopic filled with classic Sorkin walk-and-talks, thoughtful meditation on his time in office, and plenty of banter and wit—wit he hasn't gotten to flex since *Jumanji*. Oscar season rolls around and The Rock becomes the first person to win a best actor Academy Award for playing himself.

Seeing his unique position as both a Hollywood icon and a former president, The Rock creates a daytime talk show hosted by former presidents called *The Club*. Hosted by The Rock and Barack Obama, it maintains the lightness of trailblazers like *Ellen* while adding a touch of gravity rarely seen on daytime television. The Rock usually plays the moderator; Obama controls the flow of their interviews and never shies away from asking difficult questions of their guests. No talk show can compete with the sight of the two most charismatic presidents of all time chopping it up over coffee, and *The Club* earns multiple Emmys over the years.

Some years later, a life well lived comes to a close. Months after the nation finishes mourning the passing of President Dwayne "The Rock" Johnson, a series of recordings is discovered on his laptop. The Rock, it turns out, had been recording a country album in his twilight years. This news comes as a shock to everyone, even his family. More shocking is that the songs are good—better than good, even. It's one of the best albums of the decade, filled with simple, stripped-down acoustic guitar tunes anchored by melancholy lyricism the likes of which haven't been heard since Johnny Cash and Tom Waits. The album goes platinum almost instantaneously, revealing a new side to the Most Electrifying Man in All of Entertainment and Also Politics. Everyone knows it's going to win before nominees are announced. Nonetheless, a nation cheers when the People's Champion posthumously wins the Grammy for best album.

It's a shame he never got to see his goal through while alive. But at times, greatness calls on us for bigger things than we had ever planned. Perhaps the years he spent serving his country were years that could have been spent EGOTing. America will never know. Still, on some July nights, when summer storms roll through the nation and lightning flashes in the sky, children and grown-ups alike smile at the thought of The Rock. At the end of the day, the most electrifying man did good. And even if he didn't get to see it in his lifetime, generations to come will know that Dwayne "The Rock" Johnson EGOTed.

PART IV

Our Main Event: Dwayne Johnson vs. The Rock

We all have our own paths to walk. Our stories are unique, no two following quite the same trajectory. Struggle and victory alike will never find a soul the same way twice. Still, certain human experiences are universal, none more so than the moment when we ask ourselves the eternal question that everyone in the entirety of our species' short time on this floating space rock we call home has asked themselves at one point or another: Who am I?

Inevitably this question plagues us all, even the best of us. Abraham Lincoln, Leonardo da Vinci, and Michael Jordan have struggled with it. It is both the backbone of Joseph Campbell's storytelling rubric of the hero's journey and the central premise of the Disney Channel original series *Hannah Montana*. Struggles of identity are universal, which is why they're so common in stories. There's nothing more relatable than watching someone strive to figure out who they are.

This narrative of self-discovery is so compelling that we often seek out examples of it in real life. Watching an artist or athlete succeed in figuring out who they are and what they're meant to do is thrilling. Your relationship with their art and with the artist can be elevated through the process of witnessing their journey. Robert Pattinson is a singular talent whose decision to work with directors who defy film conventions is thrilling, but some of the joy of watching something as iconoclastic as *Good Time* comes from knowing that, ten years ago, he was typecast in *Twilight*. His journey from Teen Heartthrob #82 to arthouse icon is a compelling story in and of itself, and his body of work can be appreciated more because of it.

For every Robert Pattinson there are plenty of actors who fail to find their niche. Moviegoers have soundly rejected Joel Kinnaman (*RoboCop*) and Jai Courtney (*A Good Day to Die Hard*; *Suicide Squad*) as blockbuster leading men, and neither has figured out what roles work for them. A clear, concise sense of identity can be everything to an artist. It influences their projects, their approach to their craft, and how they carry themselves as a public figure.

It's hard to think of a celebrity more self-assured than The Rock. His confidence is palpable, the driving force behind every creative decision he's made for the last several years. Every role he picks, every project he launches, every T-shirt in his clothing line is a decision made with utter self-assurance. He knows who he is and, as a result, *we* know who he is.

This has not always been the case.

Not only are few celebrities as seemingly self-aware as The Rock, there are also few who have endured a crisis of identity the magnitude of which he experienced in the first decade of his acting career. The Rock came to Hollywood from professional wrestling, a carnival trade that isn't taken particularly seriously outside the sport. For years he struggled to find his voice as an actor and endured a number of humiliations that could have—or should have—broken him and absolutely ruined the semblance of a career he'd tried to build. Rather than give up, he soldiered on, trying and failing time and time again to figure out who he was as a performer and a cultural figure along the way. Was he doomed to always be The Most Electrifying Man in Sports Entertainment, not an actor but a professional wrestler with delusions of Hollywood grandeur? Would his survival as an actor require killing his past and shedding the moniker that made him famous? And in the complex moviemaking landscape of the mid-aughts, was there even room for a movie star like Dwayne Johnson?

His struggle is our own. Watching him navigate the path from pro wrestler to actor has amplified the affection audiences hold for him, and seeing him discover his purpose as a public figure has been a cathartic experience. The Rock's greatest fight was never against Stone Cold Steve Austin or Triple H, Vin Diesel, or his reputation in the wake of *Tooth Fairy*.

The Rock's greatest battle was against Dwayne Johnson.

I: The Rock

We start at the only place there is to start a story like this: the beginning. The year is 1997. A pre-Lewinsky-scandal Bill Clinton is president. It's socially acceptable to enjoy the Red Hot Chili Peppers. And the public remains polarized on one of the hottest commodities in entertainment: professional wrestling. The world of spandex and suplexes is hotter than ever, a feat accomplished largely thanks to an influx of tremendous talent both inside and outside the fabled squared circle. This is a period in which wrestling grows up, at least as much as a form of entertainment in which men and women in spangly costumes perform scripted stories while pretending to beat each other up can grow up. Admittedly much of the "growing up" involves wrestlers now being able to joke about their genitals, as if the industry is yelling, "It's not just for kids anymore!" But there's also a shift in storytelling complexity. No longer do stories in wrestling come down to Good Guy vs. Bad Guy. Moral shades of gray are used in the form of antiheroes. Villains are often authority figures, none more prominent than Vince McMahon, the WWF president (playing a fictionalized version of himself on TV). It's not exactly a James Joyce novel, but still, it's a step up from Hulk Hogan vs. Andre the Giant. During this magical era viewership hits all-time highs and public visibility of the sport and its performers is greater than ever before.

From now until the end of time, World Wrestling Entertainment (known at The Rock's debut as the World Wrestling Federation) will attempt to recapture the glory of that late-nineties boom, dubbed the Attitude Era due to the swagger of its performers and the aforementioned jokes about genitals. Even if current WWE viewership and revenue were to eclipse that of the WWF in the nineties, regaining the place professional wrestling held in the zeitgeist would be far more valuable. Professional wrestling is *everywhere* during the Attitude Era. From Stone Cold Steve Austin to Chris Jericho, professional wrestlers are rock stars. And few are as captivating, as utterly magnetic as The Rock.

He didn't start out that way. The Rock debuts in November 1996 just in time for one of the biggest pay-per-view events of the year: Survivor Series. He makes his entrance under the name Rocky Maivia, a happy-go-lucky white-meat good guy, known in the sport as a "baby face," with one of the goofiest haircuts you'll ever see and a tacky costume that mostly consists of blue streamers. His in-ring ability is passable at best, but his character is grating, bland, and boring. In the coming months his appearances on *Monday Night Raw* are greeted with thunderous "ROCKY SUCKS!" jeers from fans.

This isn't the reception the WWF brass or The Rock expect. The Rock was next in line of the great Anoa'i wrestling dynasty, a labyrinthine family tree of pro wrestlers who had defined much of the sport's history. To be practically booed out of the ring? That does not abide. Course correction is necessary. Luckily, The Rock is nothing if not resourceful.

He assumes a more overtly heelish persona, becoming one of the most delightfully hateable bad guys of the era. He's arrogant as hell, berating the audience for booing the greatness he's been so generous to grace them with and developing a slick tongue along the way. He begins to refer to himself in the third person as "The Rock." Rocky Maivia is dead and from his ashes a new star arises. Long Live The Rock.

Despite being framed as the bad guy, the "Corporate Champion" to Stone Cold Steve Austin's legendary antihero everyman, people begin to cheer for The Rock. This is a testament to his charisma and growth as a performer. He's become so undeniably talented over the past couple of years that it doesn't matter if he is the hero or the villain, because either way he's *awesome.* Thanks to this evolution, his moniker "the People's Champion," which was initially a dig that he'd whip out during his days as the evil, undeserving corporate champion, becomes a self-fulfilling prophecy. As a character, he's pure wish fulfillment, a playboy who draws heavily from legendary wrestler Ric Flair. He curries the favor of his bosses and works it to his advantage, all while wearing nice suits and expensive watches and being surrounded by beautiful women.

Everything changes on April 1, 2001, during the main event of WrestleMania 17 (stylized as WrestleMania X-Seven because it's 2001 so of course it was). That match, widely regarded as one of the greatest of all time, features what's called a double turn. The hero, Stone Cold Steve Austin, turns bad. The Rock, who starts out the match as a villain, turns good. Suddenly everything has come full circle: The Rock is a baby face again—only this time, no one is jeering. This time he's one of the most popular professional wrestlers in the world.

It's appropriate that The Rock's career in wrestling involved a crisis of identity. He was made to be the next big thing, only to realize that his version of the next big thing was outdated and out of touch. Only after finding an authentic character within himself, one who transformed the audience's jeers and boos into fuel for greatness, did he uncover something special, something that resonated with fans. The lessons learned through his journey in wrestling would save him when he made his pilgrimage to Hollywood.

One year before WrestleMania 17, in March 2000, The Rock hosts *Saturday Night Live* for the first time. His episode is well received—better than well received, in fact. Johnson credits his gig as the reason Hollywood took an interest in him. Though he'd appeared on a couple of TV shows before, even playing his father, professional wrestler Rocky Johnson, on an episode of *That '70s Show*, hosting *SNL* is the first time The Rock demonstrates that he is more than a charismatic pro wrestler. In that hour and a half he shows the world an easygoing charm, great comedic timing, and a comfort in being on camera. Soon enough, Hollywood comes calling. The Rock answers.

His first film acting role comes in 2001 in *The Mummy Returns*, the follow-up to 1999's smash-hit horror/adventure flick *The Mummy*. Johnson plays Mathayus, one of the film's villains, who is dubbed the Scorpion King due to being half scorpion. Subtle, right? Mathayus is a conqueror who sells his soul to the Egyptian god Anubis and later returns as a half-scorpion monster. Despite the fact that Johnson appears only minimally on-screen (his monstrous form is entirely CGI and *really* gets the uncanny valley senses jumping), his film debut is hugely successful and quickly leads to a self-titled spinoff prequel for his character.

With *The Scorpion King*, The Rock sets an impressive world record that puts in perspective just how hot a property he is at the time; he's paid $5 million for the movie, the highest salary for an actor's first starring role. Though the film doesn't quite capture audiences the way that *The Mummy* films did (never underestimate the power of Brendan Fraser, who sits out for *The Scorpion King*), it grosses $165 million against a budget of $60 million. The Rock is officially a successful leading man. He begins to gradually step away from pro wrestling and commit to acting.

There's a problem, though: Hollywood in the early aughts isn't exactly brimming with roles for former professional wrestlers. In fact, the idea of casting a pro wrestler in a movie is still something of a gimmick. Sure, The Rock has more raw acting talent than most pro wrestlers, but his two appearances as the Scorpion King are glorified publicity stunts. The first effectively guaranteed that his legions of die-hard fans from the world of wrestling would check out the movie. The second was more an experiment: can you make a pro wrestler a bona fide movie star?

Stunt-casting pro wrestlers is nothing new, though it comes with varying degrees of success. Even wrestlers who play iconic roles tend to struggle to find significant work afterward. Andre the Giant is a scene stealer for the ages in *The Princess Bride* and "Rowdy" Roddy Piper drops one of the most iconic lines in film history in *They Live* ("I came here to chew bubble gum and kick ass. And I'm all outta bubble gum."), but neither captured the same glory in subsequent endeavors.

In the wake of *The Scorpion King*, The Rock finds himself in an unenviable position. He's staked his claim as Hollywood's next big leading man. What now?

Middling action movies seem to be the logical next step. The Rock's next films are *The Rundown* in 2003 and *Walking Tall* in 2004, two of the ultimate "Well, this is on cable TV on a Tuesday afternoon and I don't have anything better to do" movies. In the former, The Rock plays a bounty hunter sent to South America to track down a millionaire's screwup son, played by Seann William Scott. What ensues is a goofy action romp featuring an unnecessarily fun performance by Christopher Walken. The Rock and Scott demonstrate an amusing buddy-cop chemistry that makes clear that this guy, this big lumpy pro wrestling superstar, is talented. He can play a great straight man to Scott's douchebag charm because The Rock gets how comedy works, not because he can only play a stoic tough guy. In *Walking Tall* he plays a little more straight. His character, Chris Vaughn, is every bit the stoic tough guy as his *Rundown* character, but this time there's no comic relief player to soften him.

These films aren't bad but they aren't great either, and The Rock's roles in them are mostly what you'd expect from a wrestler turned actor: tough guys who don't do much beyond dropping a solid one-liner and punching dudes in the face. These characters contain elements of the Dwayne "The Rock" Johnson we know and love today, but something is missing. In these films he's a budding flower not quite fully in bloom.

Nobody in their right mind would call *Be Cool* one of The Rock's star turns, but this 2005 gangster comedy marks the moment when The Rock starts thinking outside the box. He plays Elliott Wilhelm, a doofus wannabe actor with a goofy hairdo—his worst since his Rocky Maivia days. Nobody has seen this version of The Rock before, this actor who is suddenly unafraid to be something other than the tough guy. He takes risks, willing to be the butt of the joke and wear a bad wig if that's what the story needs. The film is a box office success but a critical failure, and The Rock's most interesting cinematic performance to date is forgotten in short order.

It's pertinent to mention that from his debut in *The Mummy Returns* through 2005's *Doom*, a cinematic adaptation of the beloved video game that was panned by critics, Johnson is billed on posters in big, bold letters as THE ROCK. The recognition of his pro wrestling identity is a huge selling point even as he attempts to distance himself from the character. It's a blessing and a curse; The Rock sells movies, but only a particular kind of movie. And the audience for that kind of movie seems to shrink with every opening weekend.

The Rock is in an uncomfortably familiar position: he's failing. His transition to Hollywood isn't going the way he'd planned. His identity as The Rock is simultaneously the only thing keeping him afloat and the biggest detriment to his career taking off.

The time has come for something new. The time has come for some*one* new.

II: Dwayne Johnson

A funny thing happens when 2006's *Southland Tales* hits theaters. Despite featuring a man who looks, walks, and talks like The Rock, The Rock is nowhere to be found. Instead, the actor bearing an uncanny resemblance to the Most Electrifying Man in Sports Entertainment goes by a startlingly normal and largely unfamiliar name: Dwayne Johnson.

The Rock is no more. Dwayne Johnson has arrived.

In retrospect, this is an admirably risky move. Former professional wrestling superstar The Rock isn't perfect, but he's a box office draw. To shed this moniker is to shed his most recognizable asset. It's akin to a comedic actor deciding they want to be taken seriously and playing, like, an alcoholic middle school teacher, or to Chris Hemsworth not taking his shirt off in a movie.

In 2006 we know The Rock. We understand The Rock. The Rock is cool. The Rock is funny, tough, charming. Dwayne Johnson? Who's that? What, is he trying to take himself seriously now? Why should we care?

Southland Tales is an unusual film for Johnson to appear in. It's unusual, period. The film is the brainchild of *Donnie Darko* director Richard Kelly, and it's as strange as you'd expect a movie written and directed by the *Donnie Darko* guy to be. For starters, the cast consists of a former pro wrestler (Johnson), two pop stars (Justin Timberlake and Mandy Moore), one former teen It Girl (Sarah Michelle Gellar), and the guy from *American Pie* whose whole thing was that his mom and his friend regularly have sex (Seann William Scott). Although the film is ambitious, it's all over the place tonally, depicting a strange alternate timeline dystopia in which, after a series of nuclear attacks, the United States is fighting in World War III. The draft, martial law, and government censorship are ever present. Through his cast, Kelly explores the dark side of the military-industrial complex, tabloid culture, and the nature of celebrity. There's a mysterious screenplay predicting the end of the world, an Amy Poehler cameo, and a split in the space-time continuum. Amidst it all, Timberlake's character performs a musical number that feels practically run of the mill.

However, there is interesting subtext in Johnson's character. He plays an amnesiac action superstar, which is rather on the nose for his first starring role outside the action genre (though similar to his character in *Be Cool*). Throughout *Southland Tales* he's chomping at the bit to make his audience forget The Rock and realize that he's capable of more than one-liners and fistfights. Aside from the role falling outside of The Rock's typical tough-guy wheelhouse, you can tell by watching him that he's doing capital-A Acting throughout. The result is a kind of abstract theatrical camp he's never delved into before.

Unfortunately, the film is a notorious flop. It premieres at the Cannes Film Festival in 2006 and is met with widespread derision. Certainly the unfinished visual effects and rough editing (the original cut screened at Cannes clocked in at 160 minutes) don't help, but they're far from the only flaws. The film receives a limited theatrical release in 2007 and then lives on only in home media.

Credit where it's due: in the years since, *Southland Tales* has earned something of a cult following. But as the first chapter of the next phase of Johnson's career, it's utterly mystifying and certainly doesn't serve its intended purpose.

Perhaps *Southland Tales* is a step too far. Perhaps something more palatable is necessary to show audiences what

Johnson is capable of. In the time between *Southland Tales'* disastrous Cannes debut and its theatrical release, Johnson stars in *Gridiron Gang*. The movie is no action blockbuster, but it's similar enough to the kind of films his existing fans turn out for. The early to mid-aughts saw a boom in middlebrow sports flicks based on true stories, from *Remember the Titans* in 2000 to *Invincible* and *Glory Road* in 2006. The genre is a safe bet, exactly the kind of bet Johnson should be placing after *Southland Tales*. *Gridiron Gang* features Johnson as a frustrated employee of a juvenile detention center who organizes a football team for the youth inmates.

It's a middling cliché of a movie. Critics note as much, though Johnson's performance as Sean Porter is widely praised. Which points to a recurring trend: Johnson turns out strong performances even in bad movies. More notable than Johnson's performance is the way he is credited—the posters and trailers advertise "Dwayne 'The Rock' Johnson." The adjustment is a small step from the Dwayne Johnson of *Southland Tales*, a sort of compromise: *I'll acknowledge my past if you keep an open mind regarding my future. Gridiron Gang*'s box office performance is mediocre, but it's enough to keep Johnson afloat until the next project. Unfortunately, just when you thought he had hit his stride, that next project brings him to a new low.

The 2007 film *The Game Plan* is bad. There's no way around that. To this day it's one of the two darkest points in Johnson's career. It is a family-friendly live-action Disney film in which Johnson plays Joe Kingman, an arrogant football star whose life is turned upside down when a little girl shows up on his doorstep and reveals that she is his eight-year-old daughter. What follows is a hodgepodge of comedic clichés and manipulative ploys to tug at the audience's heartstrings. Johnson fully commits to every inane bit, but it's all for naught. *The Game Plan* is a critical disaster—but, admittedly, a box-office success, the sort that Johnson hasn't seen in years.

Maybe this is the answer. Maybe the opposite of action star isn't serious actor but rather Disney dad. For the next few years all of Johnson's biggest roles come in family-friendly films.

Well, almost all of them. The 2008 *Get Smart* film adaptation is made for an adult audience, but it's nonetheless a mild PG-13. Johnson's character, Agent 23, is something of a throwback to his prior action hero roles. He is the international spy agency CONTROL's star field agent, an American James Bond, cool and suave and everything Steve Carrell's nerdy, meek Maxwell Smart wishes he could be. Agent 23 is perfect. *Too* perfect, even. It makes sense that a stunning (well, maybe mildly surprising) plot twist exposes him as one of the film's primary antagonists.

Agent 23 also functions as a deconstruction of action heroes. On the surface he's everything you'd expect a character played by Dwayne Johnson to be. Beneath, he's an insecure, narcissistic asshole who still isn't over his relationship with Agent 99, played by Anne Hathaway. Breaking down the action hero archetype and dismantling some of its toxic elements is something Johnson will do more effectively later, in better movies.

After *Get Smart* Johnson hits the biggest slump of his career. Between 2008 and 2010 he stars in three films that, taken as a whole, represent a creative nadir. Each is worse than the one preceding it, and with the exception of the third (which is so bad you can't help but commit it to memory) they're not even the fun kind of bad that can lead to a *The Room*–esque cult following. They're the unforgivable combination of bad and forgettable.

Race to Witch Mountain is part of a long tradition of bland live-action Disney films based on either old movies or theme park rides, alongside *Tron: Legacy*, *Tomorrowland*, and *Pete's Dragon*. Their quality varies but one factor unites them: they make zero impression on the zeitgeist and immediately fade from public consciousness as the credits roll.

The decision to make *Race to Witch Mountain* is perplexing, as is Johnson's decision to star in it. The problem isn't that the movie is particularly horrible—it's perfectly fine fodder for parents and babysitters who don't know how to keep two kids under the age of 10 content on a Sunday afternoon. It's that the whole endeavor was a zero-sum game from the jump. The film reboots a long-dormant Disney property about alien children, so ostensibly it's an IP cash-in. However, there hadn't been a new *Witch Mountain* movie since 1978 (unless you include the 1995 made-for-TV remake of the original) and moviegoers in 2009 were hardly clamoring for more. The new installment lacks franchise bait, save a brief sequel tease as the movie ends. It's nothing more than a run-of-the-mill family adventure film.

Maybe that's exactly why Johnson signs on. At this point he knows he's safe to take on family-friendly fare while he tries to figure out his place in Hollywood. His bet pays off and *Race to Witch Mountain* is a box office success. Still, it brings him no closer to finding answers to the questions of what kind of art he should be making and who he is in this new chapter. Box office success doesn't matter if it turns you into a punchline . . . and that's exactly what he's becoming. To the moviegoing public he's still the former pro wrestler, albeit now the former pro wrestler who stars in weird, bad movies. To the WWE universe, he's the guy who sold out to make *The Game Plan*.

If *Race to Witch Mountain* is Johnson treading water, *Planet 51* is the moment he goes under. Produced by Spanish animation studio Ilion, the film is voiced by an all-star cast including his former costar Seann William Scott, Jessica Biel, and Gary Oldman. At the time of production, it is the most expensive movie ever made in Spain. Johnson plays an astronaut named Chuck Baker who lands on another planet and discovers that life there is more or less identical to the American suburbs. The problem? He's an alien to them—he's basically their version of E.T. The idea of aliens in the suburbs treating a human astronaut like an extraterrestrial is a novel one that may have the makings of a good movie in it somewhere. *Planet 51* is not that movie. It's a tired collection of lazy clichés and toilet humor, an utter waste of time for all involved, including the audience. Johnson's first foray into voice acting is a dud. The movie barely makes its money back, flopping in America and turning a modest profit overseas. It's a critical nightmare and utterly forgettable, though in this instance forgettable is probably the best-case scenario. Still, the worst is yet to come.

Part of growing up is recognizing that your heroes can, and inevitably will, fail. Nobody is perfect. People make mistakes. People will let you down, people will forget to pay you back after you cover their lunch, and, in some cases, people will star in the 2010 film *Tooth Fairy*, a monumental reminder of the fallibility of our idols. Dwayne Johnson has made a number of questionable moves in his career but they all pale in comparison to this one.

This film is baffling. It defies logic, defies reason. To watch *Tooth Fairy* is to stare into the void. To watch it all the way through is to see the void staring back.

In *Tooth Fairy*, Johnson plays Derek Thompson, a hockey player whose trademark is smashing members of the opposing team so hard their teeth fall clean out of their skulls. (It's a family movie!) After he tells his girlfriend's daughter Tess that the tooth fairy isn't real, he's summoned to the world of tooth fairies and, due to his crime of being an asshole who told a six-year-old the tooth fairy isn't real, he is sentenced to serve two weeks as a tooth fairy.

Hijinks, as you might've inferred, ensue.

Let's be clear: *Tooth Fairy* is a children's movie and there's nothing inherently wrong with that. Plenty of movies and shows are made with no aspiration beyond amusing children. Not everything has to be a transcendent masterpiece that defies demographic expectations, like *Steven Universe*. Sometimes it's perfectly fine for a movie to be *Cars 2*.

But *Tooth Fairy* isn't just bad—it's cynical. Here is a movie with the right ingredients used the wrong way. Johnson, already one of the most charismatic men on the planet (even in bad movies), stars alongside comedy legend Billy Crystal and all-around legend Julie Andrews (*Julie Andrews is in this movie*). These are three of the most effortlessly charming performers of all time, and they're accompanied by the reliable Stephen Merchant and Ashley Judd. Making a decent movie starring them should be a walk in the park.

Yet *Tooth Fairy* is unwatchable. It's lazy. It's dumb. To call its humor sophomoric would be an insult to high-school sophomores across the globe. Every conceivable tooth-related pun is used at some point, and on top of that the film doesn't even make any new ones. Andrew's and Crystal's talents are utterly wasted, and although both perform their best throughout the film, even they can't elevate the shoddy script and directorial decisions.

And then there's Johnson. Per usual, his performance is not bad, but given the film's lowest common denominator material, it is inaccurate to say that he's good in a bad movie. Rather, he exists in a bad movie. He saunters through it, trying his best. But in this instance there's only so much the Most Electrifying Man in Hollywood can do.

You have to wonder why he took this project. Why was this a movie he felt compelled to lend his talents to? Did he owe somebody a favor? Did director Michael Lembeck, who afterward almost exclusively directed made-for-TV fare, blackmail him? In 2014 he opened up about some of his creative decisions in the late 2000s. Turns out, his representation pushed him to do *Tooth Fairy* and, in fact, most of the films he starred in during this family-friendly chapter. They also convinced him that, in order to distance himself from professional wrestling, he should stop hitting the gym so much. Shrinking down would help him distance himself from his time in the WWE. Like proverbial devils on his shoulder, this team steered him further and further from the actor he could become.

After the utter humiliation of *Tooth Fairy*, Johnson has had enough. No longer will he waste his prime on lowbrow family comedies. Never again will he let an agent or manager steer him from the place where he felt the most serene (the gym). The time for letting people in suits tell him who to be has passed. It is time for him to trust his gut. And so Johnson cuts ties with his representation and seeks advice from an old friend: Vincent K. McMahon, the man behind World Wrestling Entertainment. Vince puts Johnson in touch with the WME talent agency. Johnson signs with them, laying the foundation for the next era of his career.

It's time for Dwayne Johnson to come home.

Interlude: Once in a Lifetime

You will never hear a crowd cheer quite as loud as the audience in the Honda Center does the night The Rock comes home. They're ecstatic. They're enthralled. More than anything, they're surprised, though a few have caught wind of what's about to happen and lead a brief "RO-CKY! RO-CKY!" chant during the buildup. When he makes his entrance he is met with a guttural, primal scream—the sound a mass of people makes when they're witness to the impossible.

As much as a year before his return to professional wrestling, Dwayne Johnson was finally beginning to acknowledge his eternal ties to the sport. In January 2010 he was a guest on the *Late Show with David Letterman*, whose host pointedly introduced him as Dwayne Johnson. The interview strayed from the traditional path of late-night guest spots. Rather than promote a film, he and Letterman chatted at length about Johnson's connections to pro wrestling, his family history, and his career. At one point Letterman commented on Johnson's public identity: "You'll always be The Rock."

He proceeded to ask Johnson if he consciously decided to begin identifying himself as Dwayne Johnson rather than The Rock. Johnson's immediate response echoed Letterman's previous observation: "Well, I'll always be The Rock." He talked about how much it meant to him to have everyone from Colin Powell to little kids (he's usually "Mr.

Rock" to them, he said) call him that; after all, it's a pretty great nickname. But he never directly answered the question, and the conversation moved on. In retrospect, you can't help but wonder if Johnson skirted the subject intentionally. What could the answer have been? Did he decide to go by a different name at the urging of the legion of suits who steered him away from who he was? Or did those individuals capitalize on his real insecurities and crises of identity? We might never know.

What Johnson did talk about was wrestling. He seemed to miss the crowd more than anything. He waxed poetic to Letterman about the singular experience of entering the ring and seeing 25,000 people in the crowd, hearing them screaming his name. Adrenaline is a hell of a drug, and the interview makes clear that Johnson was in desperate need of a fix.

In the middle of the conversation, Johnson explicitly stated that he'd love to return to the WWE, albeit as a guest host, not a wrestler. As he did, his eyes lit up. His desire seemed so authentic.

But a year passed without that triumphant return to the squared circle. Perhaps Johnson was waiting for the right moment. On February 14, 2011, that moment came.

A week prior, Vince McMahon had hinted that the host of WrestleMania 27 would be someone who had left an indelible mark on the landscape of the WWE. Admittedly that could have been any number of people, but there was no need for such build-up if the result was going to be

Ric Flair's geriatric ass popping in for his umpteenth guest appearance to drop a "WOO!" or two.

On the night of February 14, as the lights of the Honda Center dim and the countdown to the epic reveal begins, graphics representing sizzling electricity crawl up and down the TitanTron. This is a fitting buildup for the Most Electrifying Man in All of Entertainment.

Still, even after his music starts to play, it takes the *Monday Night Raw* crowd a fraction of a second to realize who's coming. When they do, the roof of the Honda Center blows off with such force that it's probably still in orbit to this day. He walks out from behind the TitanTron and, aside from a T-shirt sporting iconography that looks like a play on the NASCAR logo, it's a perfect moment.

The man who emerges isn't Dwayne Johnson. There's no easygoing movie-star charm, no tailored suit.

"After seven long years," he begins, "finally . . . finally . . . FINALLY, THE ROCK HAS COME BACK TO ANAHEIM! Which means FINALLY, THE ROCK HAS COME BACK TO *MONDAY NIGHT RAW*! Which means, FINALLY, THE ROCK HAS COME BACK . . . home."

It's as if he never left.

The details of what happens next are less consequential to the narrative than the fact that they happen at all. In an unprecedented move, The Rock challenges the face of the WWE, John Cena, to a match at WrestleMania 28, which is an entire year away (the buildup to WrestleMania, traditionally a March or April pay-per-view event, usually begins in January). During that year The Rock makes sporadic appearances on *Raw*, hyping the match and building up the feud with Cena. Cena takes on the role of the loyal company man, calling out The Rock for leaving wrestling fans in the dust when he sped off to Hollywood. (*Tooth Fairy* is invoked multiple times.) Meanwhile The Rock lays into Cena for being a false idol, a corny poser who isn't half the icon he is.

After a year of anticipation and a tag-team match at Survivor Series, in which The Rock and Cena take on the villainous Miz and R-Truth, the big day arrives. The Rock and Cena headline WrestleMania 28, in an event billed as Once in a Lifetime. The Rock defeats Cena and rides off into the sunset.

But the story doesn't end there, of course. A year later, in 2013, The Rock challenges WWE champion CM Punk for the title and wins, becoming a WWE champion for the first time since 2003. Cena, of course, gets a rematch (nobody ever really believed it was Once in a Lifetime) at WrestleMania 29, in which he avenges his loss and reclaims the title of WWE Champion. Having finally completed the time-honored wrestling tradition of losing to your archrival before calling it quits (and finally having resolved the very real backstage tension with Cena), The Rock rides off into the sunset—for real this time. Though he makes some surprise one-off appearances, his days as a full-time and part-time wrestler appear to have ended.

Again, though, the result of what happened doesn't matter nearly as much as the fact that *it happened*. After seven long years away from the ring that took him from obscurity to godhood, from a boy to a man, The Rock came back. His reentry into professional wrestling comes with an implicit apology and promise: *I'm sorry I left. I'm sorry I pretended this isn't who I am. I promise it will never happen again.*

For the first time in years, Dwayne "The Rock" Johnson knows who he is.

III: Dwayne "The Rock" Johnson

The day that Dominic Toretto meets Luke Hobbs, the earth shakes. Their meeting is a clash between a storied unstoppable force and an immovable wall that audiences don't know they need until it's happening. The road to this moment, much like Dwayne "The Rock" Johnson's path to joining the *Fast & Furious* franchise, is a long and complicated one.

The Fast & the Furious hits theaters in 2001 and is met with tremendous success. It introduces the world to a number of new stars (who, in fact, had been putting in good work for years) including Michelle Rodriguez and the late Paul Walker. None makes a greater impression than Vin Diesel. A hulk of a man more suited to the moniker "absolute unit" than anyone else it's been applied to, he takes on the lead role of Dominic Toretto after eye-(and ear-)catching performances in other films, including *Pitch Black* and *The Iron Giant*.

In terms of narrative, *The Fast & the Furious* is nothing audiences haven't seen before. It pretty much matches *Point Break* beat for beat, only with cars instead of surfboards. Diesel's Dom Toretto is the head of an illegal street racing gang that Paul Walker's special agent Brian O'Connor must infiltrate because the gang is suspected of running a hijacking ring. As you might expect, Brian finds himself feeling conflicted by his sense of professional duty and his budding friendship with Dom (as well as his budding romance with Dom's sister, Mia).

Still, a familiar story can feel fresh with the right approach. In this case, infusing it with neon flair, a thudding hip-hop soundtrack, and an ultraquotable script full of tough-guy jargon and philosophical musings on burning rubber ("I live my life a quarter mile at a time") makes it a huge hit. *The Fast & the Furious* is the movie equivalent of a can of Mountain Dew, but somehow not in a bad way. Nothing contributes more to its allure than Diesel's performance.

Diesel is an odd bird, every bit as magnetic as The Rock but for reasons entirely opposite. Rather than refined, self-aware, and charming, Diesel is primal. He has a body carved from lumpy granite and a gravelly voice that seems to lurch up not from his vocal cords but from the earth's core. The Rock's charisma is easygoing and approachable. Diesel's is cloaked in grim mystery. Watching him in interviews, you get the impression that he hardly realizes it's there—which makes sense given that he's a lifelong Dungeons & Dragons nerd who has spent most of his career using any and all clout he's built up to get more of his Riddick (the character he plays in *Pitch Black*) movies produced. Speaking of which, Diesel taught his *Chronicles of Riddick* costar Dame Judi Dench to play D&D while they were filming together. This is in no way related to the story at hand but feels worth bringing up regardless because it would have been wild to be a fly on the wall when that was going down.

After a sequel (titled *2 Fast 2 Furious*, because it's the second one), which only Walker returns for, and a third installment set in Tokyo and featuring no returning characters except a brief surprise Diesel cameo, the original crew reunites in 2009's *Fast & Furious*. Critical reception isn't exactly glowing, but the box office success makes it clear that fans still have plenty of love for the cast and the characters, which is enough to get a fifth installment green-lit. After the fourth film ends on a cliffhanger—Dom is on a prison bus and Brian and Mia (played by Jordana Brewster) are on their way to break him out—it's clear that the follow-up has to go big. How big? About 260 pounds big.

It all happened because of a Facebook post. Early in production, writer Chris Morgan, director Justin Lin, and Diesel (who also serves as a producer on the film) write the character Luke Hobbs, a tough-as-nails DSS agent tasked with taking down Toretto and his crew. They have an older actor in mind—a Kurt Russell, Jeff Bridges type. But when Diesel notices a fan's Facebook comment saying that she'd love to see Diesel square up with The Rock in a movie one day, everything changes. Diesel latches onto the idea of casting The Rock as Hobbs, and soon enough that fan's Facebook comment becomes a reality.

It's not The Rock's appearance alone that makes *Fast Five* such a revelation, though that is certainly a major component. *Fast Five* is the point in the franchise where everything finally clicks. It's Lin's third consecutive film in the saga, and he excels at playing up the strongest elements (the familial themes, cast chemistry, and crisp photography and editing) while trimming all the fat (superfluous cast members, overly complicated plotting, and anything that dates the film, like the neon nu-metal aesthetic of the first). Short of Michelle Rodriguez's Lettie (who was killed in the fourth installment) every beloved—and relevant—cast member returns, including Matt Schulze's prickly Vince, who hadn't been seen since the first film.

Lin also harkens back to one of the key ideas of *The Fast & the Furious*: that Dom and his crew are great at pulling heists. As such, *Fast Five* is the best kind of heist flick: the "one last job" kind in which the take is so substantial that nobody involved in pulling it off will ever have to pull another job again. The plot features all the twists and turns you want from such a story, a stellar getting-the-gang-back-together montage, and, most important, a heist that lives up to all expectations.

The climactic bank vault robbery of *Fast Five* is action cinema at its apex. The bulk of the set piece consists of

Dom and Brian dragging a ten-thousand-pound bank vault, attached to their two cars via cables, through the streets of Rio de Janeiro while being chased by an army of corrupt cops and mobsters (the money in the vault, $11 million, belongs to a drug lord who runs the city). Lin's crisp photography and editing captures all the chaos and insanity of the chase without sacrificing clarity. There's little to no CGI; Lin opts instead to perform the sequence with stunt drivers so gifted that their talents border on surreal. Also, the vault replica used in many of the shots *actually weighs ten thousand pounds*. The stunt coordinators couldn't find a way to adequately replicate the effect with artificial safes or CGI. It's an all-time-great action spectacle that serves as a thrilling conclusion to an already excellent action movie.

And then there's the Dwayne "The Rock" Johnson of it all.

As Luke Hobbs, he is a force of nature descending on Toretto et al. with a singular intent: bring them to justice. From the moment he steps on-screen he's a revelation, barking orders at his team of badasses and listing his demands to the Brazilian police officer tasked with welcoming him. He's got a wry wit, cracking a dry joke or two as he goes about his business. He is unrelenting in his demands, and the only officer he allows to serve as his translator is the one in the entire city he knows isn't dirty. His debut scene is tied up with a beautiful bow in the film's use of the "one f-bomb per PG-13 movie" rule, when he tells the aforementioned officer: "Stay the f*** out of my way."

Like the first time Gaga and Bradley Cooper belt the chorus to "Shallow," a star is born.

The film deliberately keeps Hobbs and Dom separate at first, gradually building the anticipation of their first face-to-face conversation (even in their first kinetic on-foot chase they never fully occupy the frame at the same time). When they finally meet, they have a tense and wonderfully written standoff in the streets of Rio in which not a single punch is thrown. They size each other up, but Dom has the leverage and the manpower. They'll handle their business another day.

And boy, do they. Soon after, we witness the confrontation the film has promised. Hobbs literally crashes through the walls of Dom's hideout in a military vehicle, smashing Dom's iconic Dodge Charger as he does. (Subtlety has never been this franchise's strong suit, God bless it). No quips or one-liners are exchanged. It's time to throw down.

In the ensuing fight, Hobbs and Dom smash each other, as well as much of the hideout, to pieces. Their respective teammates can't intervene and only watch in horror as their friends beat the holy hell out of each other. The conflict builds to a stunning stunt in which Hobbs charges at Dom and spear-tackles him through a sheet of glass. They soar through the air and land on the ground with a thud, grappling for control. Only after Dom narrowly stops himself from lethally smashing a wrench into Hobbs's skull does the fight come to a close, and Dom surrenders. In total, two and a half minutes of screen time have passed. But those two and a half minutes make for immortality.

Hobbs is the role of a lifetime for Johnson, the character he was born to bring to life. He's a tough-as-nails badass, organically harkening back to the days of *Commando* and *Cobra*, but also the rare combination of completely self-aware and devoid of irony. Johnson and the franchise's filmmakers know that Hobbs is larger than life; Johnson mentioned in an April 2018 interview with *Rolling Stone* that "we have so much fun just coming up with the most absurd things a human can say at a moment of crisis." Yet the character never descends fully into parody or winks at the camera. As ridiculous as he may be at times, he's always grounded in a sincere pathos. In *Fast Five* his motivation is a desire to bring bad men to justice and, later, to avenge the murders of his teammates. Later in the franchise we learn that he is a single (presumably, because we never see a love interest) father to a young daughter, coaching her soccer team with the same intensity he brings to taking down drug cartels. He's a modern action icon in every way, but his debut in *Fast Five* marks the moment when audiences seem to finally realize what a special performer he is.

Dwayne "The Rock" Johnson's presence in *Fast Five* elevates the film and the franchise to levels unforeseen. It's a massive box office success—the biggest of his career and of the series alike. Suddenly Fast & Furious isn't a novelty, it's must-see cinema. Dwayne "The Rock" Johnson isn't a punchline anymore. He's not just a former pro wrestler, either. He's a damn movie star.

And it's time for him to take over the world.

Admittedly, the uptake is a little slow. Johnson spends 2011 and 2012 mostly building up to his WrestleMania showdown with John Cena and starring in only one movie, *Journey 2: The Mysterious Island*. However, his return to the WWE earns blockbuster ratings and brings attention that Johnson hasn't seen in years.

In 2013, things really start to change. Johnson opens the year with *G. I. Joe: Retaliation*, one of the more underappreciated gems in his filmography, reviews be damned. This is a film in which The Rock quotes Jay-Z in a prayer to the Christian God recited right before the Joes jump out of an airplane and kill some bad dudes. Wu-Tang Clan's RZA plays a kung-fu shaman, complete with a Shaw Brothers–style bushy mustache. In one genuinely breathtaking sequence Jinx and Snake Eyes are chased by an army of ninjas along mountainsides in the Himalayas. Most notably, The Rock and Bruce Willis team up. It's awesome. Don't let anybody tell you it isn't awesome.

Just a few weeks later Michael Bay's masterpiece *Pain & Gain* is released, a pitch-black satire of American masculinity and capitalism in which Johnson stars alongside Mark Wahlberg and Anthony Mackie. It's not as flashy as Fast & Furious or some of The Rock's higher-profile films but to this day it stands as some of the best work of his career—and, upon its release, it serves the crucial purpose of reminding audiences that he's *extremely* funny.

The year comes to a head with *Fast & Furious 6*, a box-office juggernaut that cements the series as one of the top cinematic franchises in the world. The year is a string of professional wins for Johnson, short of a reality competition show he hosts called *The Hero,* not which was renewed by the TNT network—hardly a notable loss when you're busy teaming up with Vin Diesel and Paul Walker to stop a ring of terrorists in London.

In the years that follow, Johnson embarks on an unprecedented box office tear, one still going strong to this day. Films he stars in are practically guaranteed success, from *Hercules* and *San Andreas* to *Central Intelligence* and *Moana*. As his filmography grows, we see him show us new talents at every turn. *Central Intelligence* and *Jumanji: Welcome to the Jungle* display surprising range, and *Moana* absolves the voice-acting sins of *Planet 51*. Johnson is a delight as Maui and absolutely slays his first Disney song, "You're Welcome." Yet the run isn't without failures—the 2017 reboot of eighties beach-schlock classic *Baywatch* bombs, and *Skyscraper*'s domestic performance is nothing to write home about—but on the whole, Johnson establishes himself as one of the most bankable, reliable stars in Hollywood.

And as Johnson takes Tinseltown by storm, he simultaneously branches out in other professional pursuits. In 2015 the Seven Bucks–produced *Ballers* premieres on HBO, a half-hour comedy set in the world of sports management starring Johnson as Spencer Strasmore. The show is a ratings darling and sets several viewership records for half-hour programs at HBO. The following year he partners with athletic-apparel giant Under Armour on Project Rock, a signature line of workout gear. New products are released seasonally and many, such as the Project Rock 1, his first sneaker with the company, sell out instantly. In 2017 he produces an HBO documentary about a six-month boot camp reform program for juvenile detention inmates, which provides a raw look at how the incarceration cycle chips away at young men before adulthood.

Today it's hard to recall his earlier failures, but taking his career as a whole begs the question: why this guy? Why is a former pro wrestler who starred in a lengthy series of duds the biggest star in the world? Sure, he's got that million-dollar-smile, and arms that look like they could rip tree trunks in half, and catchphrases. They all add to his appeal. But no smile can build a multimedia empire. The catchiest of catchphrases can't empower millions of people to be the best version of themselves. For a person to be as culturally resonant as Johnson requires something intangible, something primal that we all recognize, even if we don't realize it.

The Dwayne "The Rock" Johnson we know today is a man who has stopped running from himself, who has finally found himself. He embraces his past in pro wrestling. He is unafraid to be corny, to commit to the camp that is inherent in being a beloved action star. He has learned from his mistakes and will never again take on a project that requires him to apologize for who he is or who he has been. He is a man who embodies utter self-assurance even as he owns his struggles with doubt and crises of identity, the same struggles that at times plague us all.

Over the past twenty years we have watched Dwayne Johnson grapple with the same question we all grapple with: who am I? And over the past twenty years we have watched Dwayne Johnson find the answers. Perhaps, vicariously through his experience, we've found the strength to do the same.

WHICH DWAYNE "THE ROCK" JOHNSON CHARACTER SHOULD YOU TAKE TO PROM?

Wait, Trevor did *what?!* Oh my God, oh God, are you okay? Honey, I am so sorry. Okay, don't panic. Admittedly, things aren't great right now but they could be so much worse. Yes, your prom date just bailed on you. No, it wasn't pretty. Not to lay on the tough love too hard but, like, *everybody* saw this coming. Trevor is kind of a tool (his name is *Trevor*, what did you expect?) and you're, like, *way* too good for him. He was bound to screw everything up. And honestly? You're lucky it happened three days before prom and not *at* prom, you know? That would've been a nightmare.

Fortunately, we happen to know three guys who don't have dates yet. All three would make great dates depending on what you're looking for in prom night arm candy.

You seem stressed. Is it Trevor? Screw Trevor.

Wait, it's not Trevor? You're just overwhelmed? Three options on such short notice is too much, you're right.

Sorry. Tell you what, take a minute. Go home. Order a pizza. Put on *Jagged Little Pill* because, baby, Alanis knows. Then, when you're feeling up to it, don't worry about making a choice. We've got a better idea.

The following is a quiz, but not the kind with right answers because, good Lord, *that* wouldn't help decrease your stress levels. Here's what you're gonna do: Answer each question and then tally them up. Refer to the key at the end of the quiz to determine which Dwayne "The Rock" Johnson character you should take to prom.

Seriously, screw Trevor. What a dog.

1. Which of the following traits is most important to you in a prom date?

A) Someone who knows how to show me a good time.
B) Someone who is nice and courteous.
C) Someone who will extract a brutal and violent revenge upon Trevor.

2. It's not prom without a nice dinner beforehand. What are you two getting?

A) Something fancy. Prime rib, lobster, Champagne, caviar, the whole nine yards. YOPO (you only prom once).
B) Something healthy—I'm on a diet!
C) An endless banquet fit to nourish the body and soul of a warrior before battle. (Golden Corral.)

3. What's your go-to dance move?

A) A simple sway. Keep it low-key and classy.

B) Go all-out: lawnmower, sprinkler, slide, maybe even whip out the worm. Dance like nobody is watching, you know? Even though they definitely will be.

C) Is murder a dance?

4. Let's talk fashion: what'll your date wear to prom?

A) He'll be dressed to the nines: tux, boutonniere, nice accessories, freshly shined shoes.

B) Something on the casual side doesn't bother me! Tuxedo T-shirts can be kinda cute.

C) Something he doesn't mind ripping up in the heat of battle.

5. What are you and your date doing after prom?

A) Partying like rock stars.

B) Hitting up the school-sponsored Dave & Buster's after-party and trying to win a giant unicorn plush from a crane game.

C) Hiding Trevor's body.

6. Even the best dates come with baggage. Which of the following are you most comfortable with?

A) He has a mysterious past.

B) He still freezes up around the kid who bullied him in school.

C) He sold his soul to an Egyptian death god.

7. What does your date pick you up in?

A) A top-of-the-line sports car.

B) A cool motorcycle.

C) Chariot, horse-drawn.

8. You run into Trevor. What does your date do?

A) He gives Trevor his drink order. No better way to big-time your ex than to mistake him for a waiter.

B) He says something sweet but oblivious to Trevor. It kinda helps, it kinda doesn't, but it's cute so you'll be okay.

C) Your date is here specifically to run into Trevor.

RESULTS

If you answered mostly As: Your prom date is **Spencer Strasmore from *Ballers***! You like a date who's suave, smooth, handsome as hell, and, most important, knows what a good time looks like (and can afford to show it to you). You don't mind taking the backseat if it means your date is the life of the party. Sure, he might not call you back after tonight, but he'll make sure your prom will be such a rager that you don't even mind.

If you answered mostly Bs: Congratulations, you're taking **Bob Stone (formerly known as Robby Weirdick) from *Central Intelligence*** to prom! Is he a little odd? Sure, but hey, a little eccentricity never hurt. He may show up in a unicorn-print tuxedo or say something ridiculous if the two of you run into Trevor, but let's be real: you couldn't find a nicer dude to be your date. He's a consummate gentleman and completely unafraid to cut loose on the dance floor. Just cross your fingers that he's not called away on a top-secret CIA mission before the last dance of the night.

If you answered mostly Cs: Trevor is gonna feel like a real dingus for screwing things up with you when you show up to prom with **the Scorpion King**. He's gonna feel even dumber when he's challenged to ritual combat and brutally slain in front of the whole school. *So* embarrassing, right? Well, maybe he shouldn't have broken up with you. Enjoy hell, Trevor.

A COMPREHENSIVE INDEX OF EVERY TIME DWAYNE "THE ROCK" JOHNSON HAS APPEARED AS HIMSELF IN MOVIES AND TELEVISION

Celebrity cameos in movies and TV shows are nothing new, and when done well, such an appearance can make for a memorable and even defining career moment. The movie *Airplane!* is more than thirty years old and its running Kareem Abdul-Jabbar gag hasn't aged a day. The "We're not worthy!" bit in *Wayne's World*, when Wayne and Garth bow before Alice Cooper, is the film's most quoted line. Cameos occasionally even serve as image rehabilitation; nothing humanizes a movie star quite like a self-aware self-deprecating gag.

Once a star reaches a certain level of fame, a guest spot on a sitcom episode or a split-second appearence in a film (Dustin Hoffman browsing DVDs as Jack Black belts "Mrs. Robinson" in 2006's *The Holiday* is an all-time great instance of this) is likely. Some may take on a supporting role as themselves; Kareem did it in *Airplane!*, and LeBron James did it in 2015's *Trainwreck*. It only makes sense that The Rock has played himself a time or two.

In fact, the fictional character of Dwayne "The Rock" Johnson has popped up in different media more times than the real Dwayne "The Rock" Johnson has hosted *Saturday Night Live*. Is The Rock on his way to becoming one of the great multimedia characters in the grand canon of fiction, joining the likes of Sherlock Holmes, Robin Hood, and King Arthur? Probably not. But if he's taught us anything, it's that nothing is impossible for The Rock.

What follows is a comprehensive chronological index documenting every instance of Dwayne "The Rock" Johnson playing Dwayne "The Rock" Johnson in a television show or movie, followed by a brief explanation of the appearance.

1999: *That '70s Show* S1E15, "That Wrestling Show"

Our first entry technically requires an asterisk next to it. In The Rock's first guest-starring role on a TV show, he doesn't actually play himself—he plays his father, pro wrestler Rocky Johnson. The show's protagonist, Eric Forman, and his father, Red, attend a wrestling match and end up meeting Johnson backstage. In addition to The Rock playing his biological father, he says in the episode that he has a son (note: the son is Dwayne "The Rock" Johnson) who he thinks will grow up to be "the most electrifying man in sports entertainment." This is the moment in which the fictional character of Dwayne "The Rock" Johnson is born, which is why this episode warrants inclusion on this list.

2007: *Cory in the House* S1E21, "Never the Dwayne Shall Meet"

The Rock first plays himself on the Disney Channel original series *Cory in the House*. A spin-off of the hit series *That's So Raven*, the show follows Raven's brother Cory and their father, who move into the White House because the father has been hired as the president's chef. The Rock's guest spot was intended to serve as a promotional bit for his upcoming movie *The Game Plan*, which premiered a week after the episode aired. Johnson's *Game Plan* costar, actress Madison Pettis, plays Sophie, the president's daughter, in *Cory in the House*. Let's give a big round of applause for synergy, folks.

In "Never the Dwayne Shall Meet," Cory and his friends hear that Dwayne Johnson is in town and they blow off a tea party Sophie is hosting in order to try to meet him. They end up stuck in a closet and missing their chance. However, on his way to meet the president, Dwayne stumbles upon Sophie's empty tea party. There's a genuinely endearing and hilarious bit in which he introduces himself as, "Dwayne Johnson, but some people call me The Rock," to which Sophie responds incredulously, "Yeah, let's just go with Dwayne." He ends up sticking around for her tea party. It's sweet. As far as first cameos go, you could do a lot worse than this.

2007: *Hannah Montana* S2E17, "Don't Stop 'Til You Get the Phone"

The Rock followed his *Cory in the House* guest spot by dropping in on an episode of the Disney Channel show *Hannah Montana*. The episodes aired back-to-back as a sort of doubleheader to get kids extra stoked about a not-great movie, and to be fair, it worked. His role in the former was a brief, endearing bit, but his appearance on *Hannah Montana* is less a cameo and more the lovechild of a LiveJournal fanfiction and a fever dream.

Hannah Montana tells the story of Miley Stewart, a girl who is normal in every way except that she's secretly an international pop sensation named Hannah Montana (hey, that's the name of the show!). The plot of season 2, episode 17 involves Miley and her best friend Lilly trying to find a way to afford the hot new Z-Phone. (For plot reasons, Miley does not have access to the literal millions of dollars she makes as an international pop sensation.) They hatch a scheme to take an embarrassing photo of Miley in her Hannah getup and sell the photo to the paparazzi, then use the money to buy the phone. The only problem? They realize too late that Miley's necklace, which spells her real name, is visible in the photo, compromising Miley's secret identity. The tabloid that bought the embarrassing photo agrees to give it back in exchange for an equally embarrassing photo of, you guessed it, Dwayne "The Rock" Johnson.

Miley and Lilly pose as spa employees at The Rock's hotel and give him . . . less a makeover and more a drag-over. He's in a wig and a full face of admittedly well-blended makeup by the time Miley snaps the photo. But in a moment of moral crisis she refuses to leave the hotel with it, instead offering her camera to The Rock and helping him remove the makeup. In exchange for her honesty, The Rock shakes down the paparazzo to whom Miley sold the original picture. Everyone gets a happy ending.

The Rock's *Hannah Montana* appearance hasn't aged well. It's rooted in gross gendered humor and vague transphobia. However, both his 2007 Disney Channel cameos portray The Rock as a big ol' softie at heart.

2009: *Wizards of Waverly Place* S2E15, "Art Teacher"
The Rock concluded his trilogy of Disney Channel cameos with a brief guest spot on *Wizards of Waverly Place*, a show about a family of sorcerers in modern-day San Francisco. In "Art Teacher," Max, the youngest of the Russo family, pretends to have a life-threatening disease known as "mono-orangosis" in order to get attention from celebrities. One of those celebrities is The Rock, who immediately runs into middle sibling Alex (played by Selena Gomez) when he arrives at their school.

If you've never seen the show before and view the following minute of television in a vacuum, you could be forgiven for assuming Alex is a teenage sociopath. She has no idea who he is, assuming he's the plumber, and spends the majority of their minute-long interaction relentlessly screwing with him. In a genuinely baffling exchange The Rock says Alex seems "like a nice girl" despite the fact that she's done nothing but belittle him since they met thirty seconds ago. As he walks on to greet Max, whom he believes to be dying, Alex shouts, "Dwayne Johnson is here!" and The Rock is immediately mobbed by students. Again, teenage sociopath.

2010: *Family Guy* S8E10, "Big Man on Hippocampus"

Celebrities voicing animated versions of themselves on *Family Guy* is nothing new, but The Rock took it to a whole new level in 2010. The season 8 episode "Big Man on Hippocampus" features a full-on, live-action guest appearance from The Rock.

Family Guy is not, nor has it ever been, the home of groundbreaking, transgressive comedy. But if you need a good dirty joke fix, it's probably got you covered. In this case the gag occurs during a sex scene between the protagonist, Peter Griffin, and his wife, Lois. A warning flashes across the screen explaining that because the content is explicit, the show can't depict it. In its stead, the sex scene will "be simulated by Dwayne Johnson." Then The Rock appears, sitting at a table, with an action figure of each character. He wordlessly smashes them together until one flies off of the table, and then awkwardly looks around the room.

And, scene.

2015: *Jem and the Holograms*

Did you know that in 2015 a live-action adaptation of the eighties cartoon *Jem and the Holograms* was made? If you didn't, don't worry; nobody else seemed to when the movie hit screens that October. Jem and the Holograms was the biggest box office failure of the year, grossing a paltry $1.4 million in its opening weekend and placing at number fifteen at the box office. It was quickly rushed out of theaters and given a hasty home media release the following January. Conversely, 2015 is also the year The Rock starred in both *Furious 7* and *San Andreas*, which earned a combined $1.99 billion worldwide.

He also appeared in *Jem and the Holograms*.

The film was helmed by The Rock's *G. I. Joe: Retaliation* director Jon M. Chu, which is likely why The Rock agreed to the cameo. He appears in a montage reminiscent of VH1's *Behind the Music*, in which real-life celebrities including Jimmy Fallon and Alicia Keys profess their love for the fictitious band.

The film is a dud, so seek it out only if you are a die-hard The Rock completist.

2017: *Lifeline* pilot, "In 33 Days You Die"

Like *Jem and the Holograms*, you are probably at best vaguely aware of YouTube Red, the website's premium streaming service. Ostensibly made to compete with Netflix and Hulu, it . . . hasn't. Aside from *Cobra Kai*, which is a lot of fun, the platform has produced an entire network's worth of original television that nobody has bothered to watch. One of those shows is produced by The Rock and his company, Seven Bucks Productions.

The show is called *Lifeline* and takes place in a not-too-distant future in which an insurance company uses time-traveling agents to prevent the deaths of its clients. Early in the pilot, The Rock appears in a testimonial video explaining how the service saved his life. Among The Rock's cameos this stands out as a missed opportunity. How dope would it have been to watch a futuristic assassination attempt on the life of Dwayne "The Rock" Johnson, only to have it stopped by a team of black-ops agents working for a life insurance firm that can predict the future?

All things considered, his tame appearance is a bummer. It likely served to hype up interest in the series more than function as a worldbuilding tool. The hype didn't quite materialize, and the show was canceled after one season.

2019: *Fighting with My Family*

It's surprising that The Rock didn't get involved with a wrestling movie sooner than 2019—on that note, it's even more surprising more movies about the history of wrestling don't exist. The real-life lore of that industry is often more interesting than anything that takes place on-screen, from the infamous Montreal Screwjob (look it up) to the legacy of The Rock's family in the business. *Fighting with My Family*, the 2019 film dramatization of the rise of modern WWE superstar and women's wrestling pioneer Paige, is a rare exception. Not to mention, it's good—great, even. If Seven Bucks Productions, which was involved with the film from its earliest production stages, is smart—and it is—this won't be the last time the company explores cinematic adaptations of the pro wrestling world.

The Rock appears as himself a couple times in *Fighting with My Family*, playing a sort of spiritual guide for Paige and her brother Zak. He offers the siblings important advice right before their WWE tryout (to not worry about being the next The Rock and instead focus on being the next "them"). Later he meets Paige at her first Wrestle-Mania, where—spoiler alert—she's informed that the next night she will make her *Monday Night Raw* debut. It's a cool moment, although there's no telling whether it ever happened. The film plays fast and loose with pro wrestling history (Vince Vaughn's character is a hodgepodge of several real-life figures), so The Rock's scenes come with an asterisk of sorts.

That said, who cares? It's a great movie, and The Rock comes off as the ideal version of his off-screen and out-of-ring public persona. He's charming, he talks shit, and he offers a kid with a dream crucial advice. We should all be so lucky to have The Rock as our spiritual guide at some point.

PART V

Blood, Sweat, Respect: Dwayne "The Rock" Johnson and the American Dream

"I have spent my life judging the distance between American reality and the American dream." —Bruce Springsteen

Work hard, be humble. That's all it takes to prosper in America, or so they say. The American dream has been nebulously defined since the nation's founding but its essence is that hard work and a good attitude are all it takes for any person to carve out a happy and prosperous life. It has become as firmly embedded in the mythos surrounding America as the legend of George Washington coming clean about cutting down the cherry tree—an event that, appropriately, never happened.

Problematically, the American dream is inseparable from the jargon of politics. Members of Congress and presidents reference it liberally at campaign rallies, Senate floor hearings, and State of the Union addresses. They never seem to define it beyond vague terms, though. It's a placeholder for concrete sentiment and answers.

Something as fundamental to the perception of a nation deserves to be scrutinized, shouldn't it? And once you begin picking at the stitches holding the American dream together, you'll find that the threads unravel in no time at all. A fundamental facet of the way the dream is understood is a fallacy: the playing field is not even. For the American dream to apply to all Americans would require that all Americans start at the same square on the proverbial Monopoly board. They don't.

Too often Americans are sold a self-made success story by the latest Silicon Valley tech billionaire. They started in their garage, they lived off ramen for an undisclosed period, they flunked out of Harvard, and yet they managed to persevere through any and all hardships to climb their way to the top. What is inevitably omitted from the narrative is the advantages they were granted along the way, some of which they were born into. Often college tuition has been covered by parents. Family members or friends have invested the initial millions of dollars it took to get their inspirational success story started. And many of these so-called successes are men, and often white ones at that. That's an advantage in and of itself. They might not all begin as millionaires, but to go back to that proverbial Monopoly board, they're starting the game with a few houses and hotels to their name.

Few celebrities authentically embody the values of the American dream, starting from square one and making it to the top without benefiting from significant advantages along the way. When we find figures like these, we lift them up with all our might. Rare as they are, they're the sort of people we'd like the world to perceive as emblematic of what the nation has to offer, the sort of people we see as the embodiment of the American dream.

After all, people like Dwayne "The Rock" Johnson don't come around all that often.

"Growing up, I had nothing for such a long time. Someone told me a long time ago, and I've never really forgotten it. 'Once you've ever been hungry, really, really hungry, then you'll never, ever be full.'"
—Dwayne "The Rock" Johnson

On May 2, 1972, a kid is born in Hayward, California. His dad is a pro wrestler who performed under the name Rocky Johnson while his mother is the daughter of former pro wrestler High Chief Peter Maivia, the patriarch of the Anoa'i wrestling dynasty. The kid's family moves around quite a bit. He spends a portion of his childhood in New Zealand with his mother's family, and he attends three different high schools, one in Connecticut, one in Hawaii, and one in Pennsylvania.

That's a lot of change for a kid to endure, the kind of constant motion that can cause long-term damage to a child's sense of stability. By the time he's seventeen he's been arrested eight or nine times for fighting and theft, the kind of stuff adolescents get into when their lives are in a constant state of flux. His teenage years are rife with family financial struggles: his mother's car is repossessed, the family is evicted from their apartment, the list goes on. These brushes with poverty fuel some of his criminal tendencies. He and his friends steal from the strip of high-end boutique stores in Honolulu and resell the merchandise to tourists.

The constant brushes with the law soon force him to a fork in the road: he can spend his life in jail or he can try to make a change. Something has to give, the kid knows that much. But what can a delinquent teen do to challenge his grim fate? Ultimately, he recalls in adulthood, it comes down to this: "What can I control with these two hands? The only thing I could do was train and build my body. The successful men I knew were men who built their bodies."

The Rock started from the bottom. There were no favors, no rich family members to bail him out, not a single handout along the way. More than once he came close to losing it all before he had anything to lose. You can't embody the American dream if you're born into comfort; that's not how the dream works. You can't be born into the things that others strive for; the journey toward that comfort is part of the dream. The Rock's early life and lack of significant privilege are not only fundamental in making the man we know today but integral to the way he embodies the modern American dream.

"By twenty-three years old, I failed at achieving the biggest dream of my life. My ass was kicked and I was down—but not out. I refused to give up, got back up and pushed on."
—Dwayne "The Rock" Johnson

It's 1991 and the kid has done good. After relocating to Pennsylvania with his family, he dedicates himself to playing football. He works his ass off, and by his senior year he's one of the top ten defensive tackles in the country. It pays off. The kid scores a sweet football scholarship to University of Miami, where he majors in criminology. He's good, maybe even good enough to go pro after graduating, and makes the school's championship squad.

And then, in a turn so devastating you could confuse it for a beat in a fictional sports drama, the unthinkable happens: The kid gets injured. And he gets injured again, his momentum irreparably derailed.

By the time he graduates in 1995 the NFL isn't calling anymore, but the kid doesn't quit. The Canadian Football League isn't the dream but it's a start, and unlike the NFL they're interested. So he moves up north and joins the Calgary Stampeders, where he's quickly dropped to the practice squad. He spends the first two months of his tenure on the bench and then gets booted like week-old garbage. The dream is dead. Football hasn't just not worked out, it has properly kicked his ass, sending him to Florida to move back in with his parents. As the legend goes, he arrives in the Sunshine State with seven dollars in his pocket—all the money he has to his name.

Here's the part you've heard before: with nothing left to lose, the kid takes a chance and picks up where his pops left off, joining the world of pro wrestling. Upon debuting in the WWF in late 1996 he's an utter dud, but eventually he becomes one of the defining performers of his generation. Soon after, he goes to Hollywood and spends years trying to figure out his place in that world through trial and error. He makes some stinkers and bombs along the way, many of which would end the career of any other actor. But he never gives up. He works hard and soon he finds success—more than success, really. He becomes the biggest blockbuster draw Hollywood has seen in a decade. Failure finds him many a time, but he never lets it beat him.

The extent to which The Rock is seen as an indomitable success undermines how much of his career is defined by failure. From his early days as a college football player to his wrestling and film careers, he has failed often, sometimes in spectacular *Tooth Fairy*–sized fashion. To ignore this reality is to not only set an unrealistic expectation of what it takes to achieve the American dream today—failure is inevitable on the road to success—but also to minimize the unparalleled work ethic The Rock has put into coming back from those setbacks.

What's more, he doesn't shy away from his missteps or make excuses. If something goes wrong, he takes responsibility. In interviews he's refreshingly candid about the times when things haven't gone as planned. He accepted his Razzie—an award that recognizes cinematic flops—for *Baywatch* with a good sense of humor, saying that, "We made *Baywatch* with the best intentions. It didn't work out like that but I humbly and graciously accept this Razzie." Similarly, he has openly discussed career setbacks like *Doom* and *Southland Tales*; he never responds to inquiries about those films with a terse "Next question." *Skyscraper* director Rawson Thurber wrote about this tendency in a 2018 Instagram caption, saying, "He owns it on the rare occasion something doesn't work out—never seen him pass the buck or blame someone else."

The Rock personifies the American dream not simply because he has made it in Hollywood, but because he found success through constant failure, because he learned from each loss and improved himself in his next endeavor. He never let failure stop him, despite having every reason to, and now he's come out clean on the other side.

"Stay humble, stay hungry, and always be the hardest worker in the room." —Dwayne "The Rock" Johnson

Does The Rock sleep? Presumably; otherwise, human biology dictates that he'd be dead by now. (Of course, an argument can be made that The Rock isn't human but rather some sort of new heightened breed of meta-human, the next step in our species's evolution. Perhaps his kind doesn't need to sleep.) Still, consider everything he has to balance while filming a movie. A movie shoot lasts, on average, fourteen hours per day, six days a week. That famous physique, the one that he keeps in peak condition, takes time to hone, requiring hours and hours in the gym every week. There are business calls for his Under Armour line of clothing and production meetings for Seven Bucks. Let's not forget that he's also a father of three daughters and in a loving relationship. How does he do it? How does one man juggle a pile of responsibilities that makes Everest look like a molehill and still have time to sleep and, at least once a week, down some sushi and watch a documentary?

The Rock's reputation as the hardest worker in the room isn't lip service. He's one of the busiest men in the entertainment industry and somehow never half-asses a single one of his numerous responsibilities. Watch one of his bad movies and you'll find that he's never the reason it fails. He always gives 110 percent on-screen, even if everyone else around him is floundering. "He's grinding every day," said his *Fate of the Furious* stand-in Alvin Streeter in a 2017 interview with CNBC. "There's an intensity when you're working around him, and you can see it and feel it in the air. He's going 150 miles an hour every day."

Given The Rock's workload, it's remarkable that nothing feels phoned in. Every single endeavor he takes on gets the entirety of his work ethic and energy, whether it's playing a role in a tentpole film or performing "Shake It Off" on *Lip Sync Battle* or working out in the gym. When we watch him, we can see his effort and his enthusiasm. The combination is infectious, and as viewers, we can't help but get excited along with him. It's part of his magic.

"Success at anything will always come down to this: focus and effort, and we control both."
—Dwayne "The Rock" Johnson

"You're Welcome," the showstopping tune The Rock sings in the 2016 Disney animated feature film *Moana*, clocks in at under three minutes. It is the only song he sings in the movie. Don't get it twisted now; The Rock loves to sing, as evidenced by everything from his signature Rock Concerts (get it?) during his time as a pro wrestler to his Instagram stories, which often feature him launching into impromptu karaoke sessions. His voice isn't bad—his range and style evoke a slightly more refined version of a dad trying to embarrass his kids in public—but he's certainly not on par with Idina Menzel ripping into "Let It Go." Considering this, his preparation for the 2016 animated film could have been minimal. He could have asked songwriter Lin-Manuel Miranda to write something simple for his character that he could knock out in a couple of takes. He didn't.

The song Miranda wrote isn't a three-octave master class but it's challenging to perform, especially if your experience is largely limited to strumming a guitar while you croon insults at John Cena fans. The Rock had Miranda send him the song's demo and then practiced it for months, blasting it the entire time he was filming *Baywatch*, *Fate of the Furious*, and *Ballers*. He sang it in his truck on the way to work and played it over his headphones and speakers in the gym. Every free moment he could find, he tried to make himself a little bit better. "Then if I suck, I'm okay with that," he said in a 2016 interview with *USA Today*. "Because I can go to bed saying at least I prepared."

"You're Welcome" doesn't suck at all. It's a jaunty little track on which you can hear The Rock giving everything he's got. Again, it's not "Let It Go," but it is the best vocal performance he could deliver. Nobody needs to practice the same two-and-a-half-minute song for months and months on end, chasing a perfection they know will never come. The Rock did it anyway.

The Rock isn't a naturally gifted singer. He's not naturally gifted at much of anything, save for maybe flashing a great smile. Everything we know The Rock for being great at is something he started out being mediocre at.

His pro wrestling debut and the matches he put on in his first few months with the company are practically unwatchable. Rocky Maivia moves like he's wearing a weighted vest, every movement slower and seemingly more laborious than those of his peers. The catchphrase-laden charisma we associate with him isn't there. He stumbles through promos like a middle-schooler who forgot their lines in the school play. It took time, focus, and a whole lot of brutally hard work for Dwayne Johnson to find The Rock in Rocky Maivia. We now know him as a prodigal talent, a gifted once-in-a-lifetime performer the likes of whom we may never see again in the world of professional wrestling. It's easy to forget that when the Most Electrifying Man got his start, he was still an awkward boy who seemed in over his head.

The Rock's earliest acting feats are fun, sure, but nobody organized an Oscar campaign for *The Scorpion King.* His efforts before he made his big break into movies are similarly subpar, though not for lack of trying. He's awkward as hell in early TV guest appearances of *That '70s Show* and *The Net*, and he visibly stumbles through his first few leading movie roles. Performing on-screen, it turns out, isn't the same as performing as a professional wrestler, and watching his earliest films in order is like watching a man learn how acting works in real time.

By now we know how this part of the story ends, with him becoming the most successful actor working in Hollywood. But it can't be understated that when he started acting, The Rock was not a good actor. To make it to the top, he had to learn an entirely new craft at the same time he was being handed the opportunities that required him to use it. He continues to push himself, taking on roles outside his comfort zone and projects that force him to try something new. His *Baywatch* costar Zac Efron said in a 2017 *Entertainment Weekly* interview, "He just gets better as he goes, like a flower that never stops blooming." For The Rock, the work is never done. He's always learning, always planting new seeds and working hard to see them bloom one day.

"Blood, sweat, and respect. First two you give, last one you earn."
—Dwayne "The Rock" Johnson

We can no longer be so naive as to believe that the American dream is a simple and universally attainable goal. The dream, once an aspirational construct, is crumbling beneath the weight of the reality of life in modern America. A radical perspective shift has occurred, and as a culture we are initiating conversations about how your skin color, your place of birth, and who you love can affect everything from your ability to pursue your chosen career path to your apartment application. If the playing field is uneven from the beginning, then the American dream is a rigged game. In order to reclaim the dream, we must first address the constructs that have eroded it.

The lack of advantage is what sets The Rock apart from a star like Tom Cruise. It's not that the road to the top was inherently less difficult for Cruise. The lives of performers like him, Channing Tatum, or Steve Carrell are as likely to be filled with struggles and pitfalls as anyone else's. Finding success in the entertainment field is no small feat, and anyone who manages to stay at the top for as long as someone like Cruise has isn't doing so by coasting.

The Rock has achieved the same success as these men without enjoying the same privilege. The fact that he grew up in poverty, the fact that he's from a mixed-race family that moved around all the time, and the fact that he never received any of the benefits of growing up white in America matter when you're talking about the American dream. To find success equal to or greater than that of your peers as a person of color, despite economic disadvantage, after literally passing through juvenile detention centers on the way to fame, is truly remarkable.

The Rock is an iconic example of achieving the American dream because he defies the traditional definition of that dream. Half-black, half–Pacific Islander kids who face the socioeconomic disadvantages experienced by both races aren't supposed to grow up to star in billion-dollar franchises or win the WWF Championship. He's an anomaly, a contradiction of what is believed possible of lower-class citizens in the United States. In defying the norm, The Rock exposes the norm's imperfections and injustices. His success dares fans to fix the broken system he beat. No wonder people want him to run for president.

There's nothing more American than an underdog story. And strange as it may seem to paint the biggest star in the world as an underdog, The Rock has overcome countless hurdles to get where he is today. Since May 2, 1972, he has had every possible obstacle put between him and his goals. That never stopped him. He ground it out at gyms, in wrestling rings, and on film sets, developing a relentless work ethic that remains unparalleled. Through that hard work he found the success and happiness we associate with the American dream, all while staying as humble and kind as one could imagine.

The same people who embodied the American dream fifty years ago can't be propped up as its avatars now. We've become too hip to the game; we've seen behind the curtain and know how the rigging works. There's work to be done to change this system, but in the meantime, we have The Rock to show us what we can accomplish. We need only stay humble, stay hungry, and always be the hardest workers in the room. It might not get us to what we once perceived as the American dream. But it's a good start.

Afterword

It's mid-April 2018. *Rampage*, a movie in which The Rock fights a bunch of giant monsters, has just come out in theaters. It's dope, exceedingly dope, basically written to appeal to me and me specifically. I see this movie and I start thinking, oh man, The Rock is fighting giant monsters? That's the top of the mountain, man. It's all downhill from here. What else is even left for him to fight?

So much, as it turns out. There's so much left for The Rock to fight, and I know this because I went home and started thinking of other things I'd like to see The Rock fight. At this point in the story it seems pertinent to mention that I am a grown man who lives with his girlfriend and has a credit card. The next day I hit up my editor Sheilah at Geek.com and say, hey, I've got a really weird pitch for you, and if you don't want to publish it I totally understand, but just hear me out. Sheilah heard me out and immediately said that she wanted to publish my big crazy list of things I wanted to watch The Rock fight.

I'd love to pretend I labored over the piece for days, stressing about every single word, but I didn't. I cranked that sucker out in an hour. The words flowed through me as though I were channeling my own personal gospel. I gave it a quick editing pass and then turned it in.

A couple of weeks later I'm out in Manhattan with my mom and my girlfriend. It's my birthday weekend so my mom drove up from Virginia to visit me, and of course I, the grown-up with a live-in girlfriend and a credit card, decide Mom has to see Forbidden Planet, my favorite comic shop (my mom has never read a comic in her entire life and never will). While we're in the store I get a text from Sheilah telling me that the article is live on the site. Dope! It's my favorite thing I've written in ages, so just getting to share it with readers is a great birthday present in and of itself. I share the article and tag The Rock in it because hey, you never know.

Ten minutes later we leave the store, and as we're walking down Broadway on this beautiful April afternoon my phone goes apoplectic. I pull it out and all I see is @TheRock and immediately I know something amazing has happened. We stop in the middle of the sidewalk and I pull up Twitter to see that he's shared my article—not just shared it, but talked me up to his followers and tagged me.

> "Very funny read about things I should fight next from a very cool fan/comic writer," he wrote. "My personal favs are dragon, ghosts, myself, love, and the corrupt American legal system."

Holy s***.

The stretch of Broadway next to Union Square is always

busy, and given that today is Saturday, the street is like a can of sardines, but I walk over to the curb and sit down. This is the closest I've ever been to hyperventilating. As the "WHAT?!" texts from friends begin to roll in and my mom and girlfriend laugh with joy, I struggle to process what has happened. The Rock read my dumb-ass article about how I think it'd be cool for him to fight dragons and ghosts, and he didn't immediately file a restraining order. He . . . he liked it? He said he liked it? It doesn't compute.

It's one of the best birthday presents I've ever received.

Here's the thing: it's just a tweet. I know this. I know I've joked about being an adult, but I know a tweet doesn't mean you've made a new best friend. What got me was what he said in the tweet—which is to say, that he said anything at all.

I don't need to write another three hundred words on how busy The Rock is. We all know. He's a busy guy and I posted this article on a Saturday, ostensibly his day off. The two minutes he took to skim this thing I wrote are two minutes he could have spent doing literally anything else (he's The Rock; I have to believe he has options on Saturdays). The minute he spent on top of that to talk about the article and what his favorite entries on the list were? Same deal. And the thirty seconds he took to skim over my Twitter profile, notice that my bio mentions that I write comics, and mention that as well? You get it.

I don't know how much time The Rock spent reading my article and tweeting about it. I just know that it's more time than it would have taken to favorite it or just retweet it or scroll past it, casting it into the sea of what has to be a million daily Twitter notifications.

This is, to me, the quintessential Dwayne "The Rock" Johnson moment. He committed. He did more than he needed to. He had nothing to gain. I like to imagine he did it because he wanted to and because he thought it'd be a nice thing to do. It's not the first time he's chatted on Twitter with someone I know; a while back he tweeted at my buddy Dan and gave him a nickname that is absolutely the only name to which I'll refer to him for the rest of our lives.

The two minutes The Rock spent reading and talking about my work wasn't just a great moment I got to share with loved ones on my birthday weekend. It ended up being a huge creative boost. I realized I loved writing about The Rock and did it as much as possible over the months that followed. Eventually I was given the opportunity to pitch a book about him and if you haven't caught on, it worked out pretty well. Because Dwayne Johnson took a second to say something nice to me, my life changed for the better in the long term.

I think The Rock recognizes the responsibilities that come with his position and takes them seriously. But I also think he realizes that he has an incredible gift. He can make someone's day, he can offer kind words that give people the hope or inspiration they need to get through low points. His words and actions, even in small doses, can make the world a better place. And when you step back and look at the big picture, there are a *ton* of people you could say the same thing about. But not everyone puts in the effort he does to take advantage of that gift.

That's why he matters. I love watching The Rock beat up bad dudes and drive cool cars and riff with Kevin Hart as much as the next guy, but we can find someone else to do these things if need be. The Rock matters because he's stepped up where others haven't. He's looked at his incredible opportunity to make the world a better place, to make strangers happy, to change lives, and said, "Sign me up." The way he approaches this opportunity, it never seems like a burden. He takes it on with a childlike wonder that can only come from having once been in a position where he needed a hero like the one he has become.

We're so damn lucky to have him. I think we all know that. And I hope he knows that we do.

Acknowledgments

There is no *For Your Consideration: Dwayne "The Rock" Johnson* without Ivy Weir, who took a chance on me when she didn't need to and, in doing so, changed my life.

I can't fully articulate how cool it is to write your first book with a publisher you're already a fan of. Quirk Books has been doing incredible work for years now, and getting to come onboard with this book was such an incredible opportunity. I can't thank the whole team there enough, from Brett Cohen to Nicole De Jackmo to Rebecca Gyllenhaal and everyone else who helped make this experience as wonderful as it has been.

Aurora Parlagreco, Mercedes deBellard, and Ben Mounsey-Wood are responsible for how good this book looks, and they have my undying gratitude for that.

It took my parents a long time to "get" what I do for a living, but even when they didn't quite understand it, they supported me pursuing it. Shout-outs to my sister Maddy for getting it from day one.

I love movies the way I love them today because of my Aunt Bev, whom I will always love chatting about them with, even if she prefers British period dramas to Keanu

Reeves murder ballets.

Sheilah Villari gave me a platform to write about The Rock for the first time and became the first editor to trust me to deliver on my weirdest, most niche pitches. I'm a better writer for working with her and a better person for being her friend.

I couldn't ask for better partners in crime than Larissa Zageris and Kitty Curran. Developing and writing the first *For Your Consideration* books alongside them has been a pleasure. When we were first pitching the projects, I remember thinking that even if it didn't work out, I'd made two lifelong friends in the process. Instead I made two lifelong friends and got to write my first book, which is the preferable scenario.

Jhanteigh Kupihea has been the Dominic Toretto to my Brian O'Connor since this project was conceived. Working with her has taught me so much about a world I've always wanted to be a part of and I'll never be able to thank her enough for it. If we're living our lives a quarter mile at a time, I hope we're in parallel lanes for years to come.

Danny Lore talked me down from the ledge when I was fully bugging out over whether or not this book would get picked up. They also provided invaluable insight and editorial advice when I wrote my first pitch samples.

A quick lightning round for some of the friends who got me through the months I spent pitching and writing and stressing over this project: Ryan Cady, Vita Ayala, Robert Wilson IV, Chris Sims, Cameron DeOrdio, Samantha

Weiner, Franki Jester, and Holly Aitchison, I love y'all and appreciate you staying in my corner.

I can't imagine what it's like to live with a significant other while they're writing their first book. I'm sure it isn't easy but you wouldn't know it if you saw my girlfriend Kerin over the last few months. The support, patience, and love she's given me while I wrote this book kept me afloat, and watching her create some of the most magnificent art I've ever seen alongside me inspired—and continues to inspire—me daily. Also, she didn't know The Rock and Vin Diesel weren't the same person until she saw them on-screen at the same time in *Fast Five,* which has given me a go-to party story for the rest of my life.

Lastly, Dwayne "The Rock" Johnson is my hero. He also gave this book his blessing. I wouldn't want to write it if he hadn't. Thanks, DJ.

Timeline

Important dates in the life and career of Dwayne "The Rock" Johnson

May 2, 1976: Dwayne Johnson is born in Hayward, California.

1995: Johnson signs with and is subsequently cut from the Calgary Stampede football team.

November 16, 1996: Johnson debuts in the World Wrestling Federation (WWF) as Rocky Maivia at Survivor Series.

February 13, 1997: Johnson wins his first Intercontinental Championship.

August 1997: Johnson returns from injury and turns heel, taking on the moniker "The Rock."

November 15, 1998: The Rock wins his first WWF Championship.

April 1, 2001: The Rock and Stone Cold Steve Austin headline WrestleMania X-Seven and put on one of the most acclaimed wrestling matches of all time.

May 4, 2001: The Rock makes his big-screen debut in *The Mummy Returns.*

April 19, 2002: The Rock has his first theatrical starring role in *The Scorpion King.*

January 30, 2003: After a brief hiatus, The Rock returns to WWF for what will be his last run as a wrestler for a while.

September 26, 2003: *The Rundown* premieres.

2004: The Rock's contract with the WWE (formerly the WWF) expires, ending his first run as a professional wrestler.

April 2, 2004: *Walking Tall* premieres.

June 7, 2005: *Be Cool* premieres.

October 21, 2005: *Doom* premieres.

September 15, 2006: *Gridiron Gang* premieres.

September 28, 2007: *The Game Plan* premieres.

November 14, 2007: *Southland Tales* premieres.

June 20, 2008: *Get Smart* premieres.

March 13, 2009: *Race to Witch Mountain* premieres.

November 20, 2009: *Planet 51* premieres.

January 22, 2010: *Tooth Fairy* premieres.

August 6, 2010: *The Other Guys* premieres.

November 24, 2010: *Faster* premieres.

February 14, 2011: The Rock is announced as the guest host of WrestleMania XXVII, and he returns to the WWE for the first time in seven years.

April 3, 2011: The Rock hosts WrestleMania and interferes in the main event.

April 4, 2011: The Rock vs. John Cena is announced as the main event of WrestleMania XXVIII, which will be held one year later.

April 29, 2011: *Fast Five* premieres, introducing The Rock to the Fast & Furious film franchise.

February 10, 2012: *Journey 2: The Mysterious Island* premieres.

April 1, 2012: The Rock and John Cena wrestle in the main event of Wrestlemania XXVIII, billed as Once in a Lifetime.

January 27, 2013: The Rock wrestles CM Punk at the Royal Rumble and wins the WWE Championship for the first time in nearly a decade.

February 22, 2013: *Snitch* premieres.

March 28, 2013: *G. I. Joe: Retaliation* premieres.

April 7, 2013: The Rock and John Cena have their rematch at Wrestlemania XXIX.

April 26, 2013: *Pain & Gain* premieres.

May 24, 2013: *Fast & Furious 6* premieres.

July 25, 2014: *Hercules* premieres.

April 3, 2015: *Furious 7* premieres.

May 29, 2015: *San Andreas* premieres.

June 21, 2015: *Ballers* premieres on HBO. Johnson is an executive producer and stars as Spencer Strasmore.

June 17, 2016: *Central Intelligence* premieres.

November 26, 2016: *Moana* premieres.

April 14, 2017: *The Fate of the Furious* premieres.

May 25, 2017: *Baywatch* premieres.

December 20, 2017: *Jumanji: Welcome to the Jungle* premieres.

April 13, 2018: *Rampage* premieres.

July 13, 2018: *Skyscraper* premieres.

February 22, 2019: *Fighting with My Family* premieres.

August 2, 2019: *Hobbs & Shaw* premieres.

Look out for these other titles in
the *For Your Consideration* series

Keanu Reeves

Available now wherever books are sold

The Chrises

Available in May 2020

Maya Rudolph

Available in Fall 2020